The Year-Long Day

The Year-Long Day

One Man's Arctic

by A. E. Maxwell and Ivar Ruud

Photographs by Ivar Ruud

THE TRAVEL BOOK CLUB
LONDON

First published 1977 by Victor Gollancz Ltd

The Travel Book Club
125 Charing Cross Road
London WC2H 0EB

This edition 1978 by arrangement with
Victor Gollancz Ltd

Printed and bound in Great Britain by
REDWOOD BURN LIMITED
Trowbridge & Esher

To Fredrik

Contents

Illustrations

Afternoon

Far out on the slate-blue water, amid glacier calves floating low and cold and translucent, the governor's ship began to move. The man on shore could not hear the big diesels over the wind and waves rushing against Hornsund Fjord's rocky beach, but he could see the ship come about slowly and head west, toward the mouth of the fjord and the Arctic Ocean beyond. Next summer, when the ice broke up again, Ivar Ruud would search hungrily for the first sign of the returning ship, but today he did not regret the disappearance of human company. He was ready to be alone.

There was no time to savor the feeling of freedom. Not yet. Not until his supplies were safe from the August whims of high Arctic weather. He flexed his back and shoulders, testing his tiredness. He had not slept in twenty-four hours, and the last ten hours had been spent hauling more than two tons of heavy crates and bags from ship to rowboat and from rowboat to beach.

Ivar's legs and feet were cold where water had topped his rubber boots as he unloaded the yellow rowboat. Usually he could unload just below his cabin, but a late summer wind had herded glacier calves and fractured ice floes onto the north shore of Hornsund Fjord. At another time he might have admired the ice glowing in the slanting sunlight, a necklace of baroque pearls and rough diamonds laid along the land. But at this moment he cursed the ice for all the extra work it made.

He had searched the shoreline for a mile on either side of Main Cabin before finding a place where he could land. Ironically, the only ice-free beach was beside one of the glaciers that had been so busy sending calves out to sea.

View across Main Cabin bay.
Hans Glacier and Missing Mountain
in background

From far out over the water, a pitch above the sound of the wind, Ivar heard a last salute from the ship as it moved out against the tide. One blast on the air horn: Good luck; see you in a year; good hunting. And then quiet, but for the wind and chunks of ice mumbling together as they rode the waves.

He turned to the waiting pile of supplies. He had carefully packed them into loads of approximately 100 pounds, as much as he could comfortably carry—not expecting to have to carry each load a mile. A year's amenities like books and margarine and Scotch, necessities like guns and medicine and skinning knives. The wooden case of guns and ammunition went into the cabin first. Without that case, the rest was meaningless.

Out of old habit Ivar glanced around him, watching for the swift creamy shadow that could be a polar bear. *Ursus maritimus* usually went north with the pack ice in summer, but Ivar had to be wary of the occasional bear that stayed behind. Such bears became as much scavengers as predators, but were no less formidable for the change.

After a last look around, he settled the awkward gun case into carrying position and walked toward the cabin. As he moved slowly up the mile of shoreline, a large German shepherd came running·down the rocky beach to greet him. Naika looked him over with alert dark eyes, shook a shower of icy sea water over his legs and dashed back to rejoin the huskies at the cabin. On the way, she made several splashing detours into the surf.

The distant huskies ignored Ivar for now. They had attention only for the tantalizing scent trails around the cabin. He had expected nothing different. His summer holiday in Norway had meant the huskies' imprisonment in Longyearbyen, the nearest settlement on Spitsbergen Island. While he drank beer and learned again to talk to other human beings, the huskies grew restless and surly behind kennel fences.

The trip back to Hornsund was hardly a treat for them, either. After long hours in the ship's dark hold, the five huskies emerged confused and defensive. To prevent their capsizing the small rowboat, Ivar put Svarten, the leader, on the bottom of the boat. As long as Svarten was there, the other dogs would stay in the boat. As insurance, he put Surly and Bumpsa on top of Svarten and tied them to the oarlocks. Naika and the last two huskies went on top of the pile. There were flashing teeth and rumbling growls, but no bloodshed. When Ivar started the engine, the pile of dogs subsided into quiet seething and random yips.

The arrangement held almost all the way to shore. Then the boat began rocking as the pile shifted and heaved. Svarten's head surged up under Naika's chest; his amber eyes focused on the shore. Ivar knew he had only seconds before Svarten's fight for freedom would become wild enough to capsize the boat. As Svarten lunged onto the top of the pile, Ivar shut off the engine, cut loose the dogs he had tied and hung onto the gunwales.

Svarten hit the water first. One of the huskies clawed over Ivar, frantic to follow his leader. Naika and the other three huskies went overboard in a huge splash. The rowboat bucked and rocked but did not roll over. He waited until he counted six dark heads moving toward shore; then he started the engine again.

By Ivar's third trip with a load of supplies, the huskies had worked off their first excitement and were slowly quartering the area around the cabin. Svarten marked cabin corners and other salient points with a few drops of urine, warning all comers that this territory was occupied. He disciplined the more aggressive males, but none of the fights drew blood; the huskies had no real doubts as to which dog led them. Svarten was a magnificent animal, black and buff and swift and young, a born runner.

When the huskies finally had matters settled to their satisfaction, they noticed their empty bellies and came trotting back to Ivar. They even submitted to the collar and chain in order to be fed. After the supplies were safe inside the cabin, he would free them again, but the last thing he wanted was a pack of hungry huskies rummaging in his provisions. Naika gave him a hurt look when he chained her, for normally she ran free.

Ivar started back for another load, moving with the unconscious grace of a man who knew and used his body completely. His dark hair glinted auburn and gold in the afternoon light, and his eyes echoed the shifting hues of floating ice. But unlike ice, Ivar's eyes were alive, endlessly measuring and appreciating the land around him.

To his right the gently swelling sea washed over flashing pieces of ice. Ahead to his left, Hans Glacier glimmered weakly under its summer crust of gravel and dust and rotten ice. Behind him, Main Cabin and the huskies were dark against the umber land. And around him the mountains, always the mountains, silent chiseled heads lifting above primeval robes of moss and lichen and ice. Nothing moved but the wind and waves and Ivar.

First the guns, then the food, then the books, then the rest of the supplies must be carried to the cabin. The rock salt and coal would be covered with a tarpaulin and left where they were for awhile, but even so he had at least fifteen round trips, or 30 miles, to walk, 15 with nothing to carry but his increasingly tired body, 15 with ever heavier 100-pound loads.

He shouldered another load and headed for the cabin, walking slowly, a man of medium height and immense determination.

By the sixth trip he was too tired to curse the rocks that rolled perversely under his heavy feet. By the eighth, he had stopped carrying his rifle. By the eleventh, he was an auto-

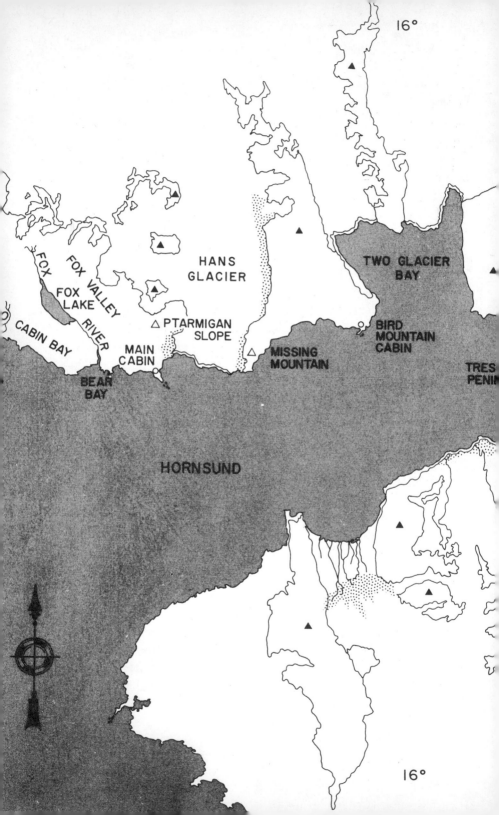

STORBREEN

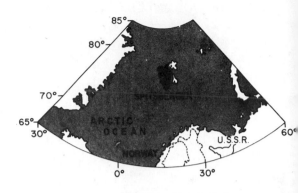

SVALBARD ISLANDS

SEVEN GLACIER BAY

HORNSUND PEAK

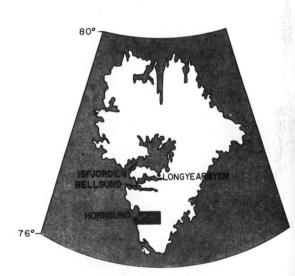

SPITSBERGEN ISLAND

○ CABIN
△ MOUNTAIN
▲ MOUNTAIN RANGE
= GLACIER FRONT
⸬ MORAINE

maton; except for the part of him that watched for white shadows, he was effectively deaf and blind. The only real memory he had of the final mile was weary relief when he dumped the last 100-pound load on the cabin floor.

Sleep dragged at his body, but he could not give in yet. There were a few small things to take care of. Household chores. Though he had been gone only six weeks, Main Cabin had paid for his absence. A storm had stripped a swath of tar paper off the roof over the storeroom, and the exposed planks had leaked generously.

Even at that, the cabin looked better than the first time Ivar had seen it. It had been built in 1957 for scientists who lived in Hornsund for a few months during the International Geophysical Year. At the end of summer, the cabin was abandoned and had stayed empty for a decade, testimony to the wastefulness of wealth—such a cabin for a few summer months. When Fredrik Rubach and Ivar had come to Hornsund three years ago, the long, shedlike cabin was a wreck; polar bears had ripped off doors and smashed in windows, allowing storms free entry. But the basic structure was still sound. After a lot of repairs, the cabin had served them well. Fredrik no longer used Main Cabin, preferring to live instead farther north at Cabin Bay, beyond Hornsund's wide mouth, on the shores of the stormy Arctic sea.

Ivar shivered in the damp and cold inside the cabin walls. He gave the iron stove a long look. As he expected, it was bright with rust despite its heavy coat of oil. But rust or no, the stove would heat, and heat would dry out the living quarters. The roof of the storeroom could wait until he had slept, but if he did not get the living room dried out, he would lose a year's supply of flour.

Work, work. And work. There was never a lack of something to do, just a matter of deciding what could not wait.

After a time, the priorities sorted themselves out automatically. But right now, Ivar had to get organized.

I've been away too long. I've become used to warm houses and stores and machines to do the work. Get your butt moving, lazy man. The ice is coming. It will be dark before you're ready, three months of dark.

He rubbed his beard stubble and smiled at his silent dialogue. He was feeling very much at home, talking to himself again—and answering. A good sign. In the best of times on Hornsund, there were three of him, two for conversation and a third to stand guard. Now, if he could just come up with a fourth, he could learn bridge. . . .

He stretched and shook the aches out of his arms. And shivered again. He could have fired up the stove when he brought the first load from the beach, but getting the supplies under a roof was more important than creature comfort. Now the perishables were safe and the creature was damned uncomfortable.

He needed fire, and so did the cabin. After weeks without dry heat, ceiling, walls, floor, furniture, everything was coated with cabin sweat. The sweat turned into hoarfrost when the temperature went below freezing, but even the high Arctic thawed in summertime. All exposed metal was a garish orange. For most of the metal, rust was merely an aesthetic problem. The stove was another matter. Because of its repeated heatings and coolings, the stove was most vulnerable to real damage.

Ivar had given it a coat of blubber oil before he left. Not high-grade machine oil, to be sure, but just as effective. He had also laid the fire before he left, driftwood kindling topped with a layer of coal. Now all he needed was some blubber on top. As the wood burned, the blubber would melt into the coal and the coal would burn hotly. By the time the blubber was spent, the coal would be able to sustain its own fire.

The only blubber available, short of going out and peeling a seal, was the cache of dog food he had left over from last year. He climbed up on the cabin roof where he kept the cache. Most of the seal carcass was still there. With a determined effort not to smell the rotting flesh, he carved off a slab of blubber. In a few weeks at most, he would have to get fresh seal for the dogs. Not that his huskies disliked high meat; they relished it. But the seal was a small one. Barely enough remained for two weeks, or perhaps three if the dogs went on short rations. He would have to go seal hunting sooner than he had planned.

Grasping the blubber firmly, he descended the ladder and went back inside. He quickly oiled the stove and put the remainder of the blubber on top of the coal. He lit the fire, unconsciously holding his breath. He was used to the odor of old blubber burning, but this slab was really rancid.

He fought the smell for half an hour, then gave up. He stoked the stove to bursting and retreated to the tiny shack he used as a bolt-hole. There were always enough supplies in the shack for an emergency trip to his Bird Mountain cabin, if he should lose Main Cabin to fire or storm or polar bears.

The shack was damp and cold and decrepit, but it was better than the frigid mist outside. And it certainly smelled better than the cabin. He curled up in clammy blankets and slept.

By the time he woke up, both the cabin and his thoughts were sweeter. The sun was up, of course. The sun was always up during the months-long Arctic afternoon. The dogs were also up—and hungry. Ivar fed them, and himself, before he tackled the remaining ton of coal and salt. The tide had taken away much of the shore ice; he could use the rowboat instead of his back for hauling. He looked at the empty shoreline gratefully. His body felt as though he had slept under a glacier. But once he was moving again, his muscles would loosen up.

A meal, a little more rest, a lot more work, and the supplies were all under a roof. Now . . . the other cabin, while the wind was still on his side. The fjord was nearly clear of ice; he could unload supplies practically at the doorstep of his Bird Mountain cabin—if the wind did not shift.

Maintaining and supplying two cabins made for logistical difficulties. Main Cabin was about 7 miles inside Hornsund's mouth. Bird Mountain Cabin was over 9 miles farther east, close to the fjord's inland terminus. A man traveling on foot or skis or dogsled could take hours to cover a single mile, especially when the weather fell apart. Along Hornsund's rugged length, a map mile became at least 2 walking miles, and sometimes 3. But the extra cabin was well worth the extra trouble. The wider his range, the greater his chances of taking fox and polar bear. He could have camped out during his hunts, but a tent or a snow cave was a poor substitute for cabin walls, and it was far easier to stock Bird Mountain's provision shelves in summer than to carry a backpack full of food through winter storms.

Most important, during the long night of winter, when his mind was both not enough and too much company, when "cabin fever" was not a joke, he simply fled to a different cabin.

Within a short time he had the boat loaded with food and tar paper and a few lengths of cut pine board. He launched the boat and pointed it directly out into the fjord. After a mile or so, he would turn east, toward Bird Mountain and the steep headlands that overlooked the chill fjord.

Above, high overhead, the distant calls of white-cheeked geese poured down on him, and their bodies made clean black lines against the cloudless sky. Ivar watched them for a few moments, envying their flight and warm feathers and air of majestic ease.

The sea hissed gently as it was divided by the yellow prow of the boat. The water hissed less gently as it met the obstruction of barely submerged rocks. Though Hornsund was a wide and lovely fjord, it had more than its share of teeth. Rock reefs and sea stacks paralleled the shoreline out to a distance of a mile. And ice was always a hazard, even in the warmest summer months.

In spite of his impatience to see how Bird Mountain Cabin had weathered his absence, Ivar guided the boat slowly toward deeper water. Hornsund did not take kindly to haste. Even if the temperamental outboard kept chugging, the trip would take nearly three hours.

As the boat nosed among the rocks, eider ducks scattered before it, filling the air with their nasal complaints. The eiders were fat and healthy and very female in their muted brown brushed with white and black speckles. There were no drakes among them. The males abandoned the females as they laid eggs, and there would be no reconciliation until next breeding season.

Nor were the males missed; any duck without offspring automatically helped her sisters care for their young. If a glaucous gull threatened a duckling, the nearest female would rush forward and seize the gull with her blunt, powerful bill. If the gull could not win free, the avenging duck dove down into the lightless sea. Long before the duck surfaced, the careless gull would be dead.

But there were no gulls threatening now; everywhere the younger eiders paddled in loose groups, thoroughly at home on the roller-coaster sea. In a week or two, the ducklings would be fully fledged, well able to look after their own needs. Then Ivar would hunt, sure that in killing the ducks he would not also be killing their offspring.

Sentimental? Perhaps, but he could afford to be, now. Like the ducks, he was fat and healthy. If he were not, his self-im-

Hvitkjinn *(white-cheek) goose*

posed rules would change. He would kill whatever he could, any way he had to, with no regrets.

Even with a normal swell and friendly wind, he was a long time picking his way through the reefs that fringed the Main Cabin peninsula. Most of the rocks that jutted out of the sea carried on their rough backs a few pale-feathered glaucous gulls. They watched Ivar with brilliant yellow eyes, confident of their own safety.

Once through the reefs, he opened up the throttle and headed out to the center of the fjord. For the next 3 miles he scanned the sea, hoping for a glimpse of beluga whales on their way down to the closed end of the fjord. But he saw none of their gliding white shapes this time, not even so much as a sudden gush of silver breath condensed above the dark lifting waves.

But he did spot game. The slick brown head of a ringed seal broke water 30 feet off the bow. Round dark eyes watched Ivar for an instant, then vanished beneath the sea. Immediately, Ivar shut off the motor, raised his rifle, and waited motionlessly for the seal's return. The huskies needed food and his fires needed oil; that sleek brown flash represented 200 pounds of meat and blubber. The rowboat lifted and fell and lifted and fell as Ivar sat noiselessly, his light-blue eyes scanning the sea for a shining dark head.

There—20 yards to the right.

Ivar aimed smoothly, quickly, and just as quickly decided no, not this time. Too easy to miss in the rolling sea, too easy to kill instead of stun, and if he killed, the seal would sink before he could reach it. The seal's death would be wasted.

Ivar set the rifle aside and started the motor. In a few weeks, when the ringed seals' blubber thickened against winter and the glaciers no longer diluted the buoyant seawater, dead seals would float, and hunting would be easier. His huskies could not wait that long, but he would have other chances, better chances, to take a ringed seal.

The boat wallowed slightly, then slid into a course parallel to Hornsund's north shoreline. Ivar still watched for telltale patches of foam, but the danger from rocks and reefs was not so great here as closer to shore. He had time to look back at the ragged slice of land that was home.

Even with light and good weather and a machine doing all the work, Hornsund seemed huge. Most maps showed little dots for the Svalbard Islands, and Hornsund Fjord—if it showed at all—was a nameless slit in Spitsbergen's lower half.

But maps were only one kind of reality. Mapmakers floated by the islands in a ship or flew over in a plane, cameras clicking. Ivar used their maps, understood their limitations, and laughed or swore over the mistakes he found.

Just east of Main Cabin there was a beautiful twin-peaked mountain. In summer the peaks were a deep chocolate color, and along the mountain's west side Hans Glacier grumbled to the fjord. A hard landmark to miss, but one mapmaker succeeded. Ivar called the error Missing Mountain. Other mapmakers had found and named it Fannytoppen, but it would always be Missing Mountain to Ivar.

He did not hesitate to give personal names to Hornsund's landmarks, names such as Fox Valley and Goose Bay and Bear Bay and Omelet Slope and Sonofabitch Pass. Where the mapmakers flew or floated, he skied or walked or crawled. His Hornsund was different from theirs, and he knew the area far more intimately than they did.

Yet he had almost missed knowing Hornsund at all. The Svalbard Islands, of which Spitsbergen was one, were under the administration of the Norwegian government. Before Ivar could hunt or trap, he had to receive permission from the government. When he first came to Longyearbyen, the governor of Svalbard refused to grant that permission. The reason given was that Ivar was ill prepared to meet the exigencies of the high Arctic.

Ivar disagreed, loudly and at length, with the governor. It was futile. Ivar was only nineteen and, as he later realized, tactless. Nothing in his life had prepared him to deal successfully with the proud obstructions of a bureaucracy. When he was fourteen he had left home, over no one's objections, and lived on the streets of Oslo with children older but no wiser than he was. As soon as he turned fifteen, he joined the merchant marine. He saw Rome, Paris, London, New York, Rio de Janeiro—and most of the whores and bars between. It was all very exciting for a Norwegian farm boy.

There was a problem, though. Ivar was 5 feet 8 inches tall, weighed 140 pounds and was touchy about his size. In time, he learned that fighting had no future. The last lesson came in a Brazilian bar. Two crews were there, Ivar's and one from another ship. He was not sure how that fight started, but it was fast, ugly and final. The bar was destroyed. Not a chair, not a bottle, not a glass was left intact. Nothing. He crawled out of the wreckage very sober and grateful to be moving at all.

It was the first time Ivar had ever been pleased to be alive.

By the time he signed on for the last Norwegian whaling expedition to Antarctica, he had learned to control his temper. For seven months he saw only the ship and other men. No ports, no women, no time off. The months would have been endless if he had not met Fredrik Rubach. Fredrik had lived on the Svalbard Islands for many years and enjoyed talking about his experiences. Ivar enjoyed listening. By the end of the expedition, they had agreed to be partners for a year of trapping on Hornsund Fjord.

Ivar still wondered why Fredrik had wanted him as a partner. Fredrik had enough money and more than enough experience to trap by himself. Ivar knew the older man preferred trapping alone. The only possible answer was that Fredrik liked Ivar. At the time, Ivar found that hard to believe; no one else liked Ivar back then, including himself.

The plans they made led them to Longyearbyen—and the governor. Ivar had purchased all the supplies Fredrik's years of experience said were necessary. The governor had a different list.

A bedpan was high on his list. What would happen to poor Ivar if Fredrik were at one cabin and Ivar were at another, injured or too sick to get up and use the honey bucket? Ivar pointed out that if all that happened, a smelly bed would be the least of his problems. The governor said Ivar must, repeat must, have a bedpan. There was not even one bedpan for sale in Longyearbyen, and no time to ship one in from Norway.

The bedpan was only one of many obstructions. When Ivar should have been repairing cabins and fixing traps and hunting food for Fredrik and himself and the dogs, he was shadowboxing with the governor's rule book.

He lost, of course. As the ice congealed around Longyearbyen, he sold his provisions at a loss and took the last ship out. On the way to Norway, he planned ways to earn enough money to try again. Then he was drafted. Two years of shoveling snow for the greater glory of Norway.

But Ivar was stubborn. As soon as he was discharged, he started buying provisions. Instead of waiting until he reached Longyearbyen for clearance to trap, he took care of the paperwork in Norway. At least the bureaucrats in Oslo understood that Ivar knew as much about surviving in the high Arctic as their rule books. One man even told him that it was his own ass, and if he wanted to freeze it off, that was his problem.

And now, at the beginning of his fourth year here, he understood better why the governor had been so reluctant to turn an inexperienced youth loose in the Arctic. Hornsund can be an unforgiving place. At 77 degrees north latitude, less than 400 miles from the North Pole and over 100 air miles from the nearest town, Longyearbyen, Hornsund was no place for fools. The wind and cold were intense, the mountains swept clean of all except moss and lichen, rock and ice. The biggest tree on the island was an 8-inch-high birch.

A sudden barrage of noise rose above the sound of the engine. Ivar looked away from the land and back to the sea. Up ahead, several square miles of sea were churned silver. The dovekies were fishing.

They were amazing birds, like white-bellied bats, smaller than his hand, yet they dove deep into the cold sea in search of prey. Dovekies bred in their millions in the talus slopes of Hornsund, their nests in burrows hidden from foxes.

And the noise those little birds made—a high, very rapid trill that poured out of them and was multiplied into an incredible cacophony. Yet the dovekies were beautiful to watch, tiny feathered divers in clean black-and-white, scattering silver water from thousands of dark wings.

Ivar shifted position almost unconsciously; he had been sitting on a hard, narrow plank for almost two hours. His muscles were stiff and his feet ached with cold as he flexed his toes inside his boots. Only an inch beneath his feet was water that never varied more than a few degrees from freezing. The cold that seeped through yellow hull and rubber soles could be driven out only by fire or exercise. As both of those were at least an hour away, he resigned himself to discomfort. He knew it would be worse before it would be better.

The northern shore slipped quietly astern, a pageant of mauve tundra, knife-edged gray mountains and gleaming ice. Ahead, the great stone pyramid of the Bird Mountain massif rose above the blue-green sea. At the base of sheer cliffs, a tiny peninsula crept out into the fjord. Ivar's cabin was still hidden on the far side of the peninsula, but he picked up the binoculars and stared ahead intently. He had prepared both cabins as well as he could against polar bears and storms, but tourists were another matter.

Even when they remembered to shut the door, they did not always leave empty-handed. Not that the tourists took much. By their standards there was not much worth taking; a small mirror, an odd spoon, Norwegian flowers he had dried and nursed intact to Hornsund.

He could live without seeing his face and he could stir his coffee with a knife, but those dried flowers . . . in the long winter darkness when he hungered for sun, he had nothing else to recall the gentle fields of summer.

Some of the tension left him when he finally saw the cabin —closed door, window shutter in place, no obvious damage. He beached the boat, grabbed his rifle and the roll of tar paper and trotted toward the cabin. He was stiff and somewhat clumsy from cold, but he hurried anyway. He would not feel at ease until he had checked the cabin's interior.

The Bird Mountain cabin had begun as an overnight shack, hardly more secure or spacious than a one-man tent. During his second year in Hornsund, Ivar had rebuilt and expanded until a rough shack became a snug home. The cabin was still small, a 12-by-6-foot rectangle divided into two equal rooms, only one of which was heated by the stove.

The first room was used for storing provisions, fuel, guns and tools. The door, as all outer doors in snow country, opened inward. There was a hinged panel in its upper half. The small room had not been disturbed. He propped the tar paper on its shelf, put the rifle in its rack, then backed up to the center of the room in order to open the living-room door. Other than an arc for the door and a narrow passage from the outer door, the storeroom was completely full.

Bird Mountain Cabin, summertime

The living room had little more free space. Its 6-foot-square area was taken up by a bunk, table, washbasin, chair and stove. Except for one place beneath the window, the walls were covered with cabinets and shelves. A quick glance around reassured him that everything was as he had left it, except that the stove was rusty.

He oiled it with old blubber scraps, started the fire and fled back to the boat. The escape from the stench was only temporary; he had more supplies to bring up to the cabin. He unloaded the boat methodically, ammunition and perishables first, coal and cut wood last. The storeroom shelves had a scattering of leftover flour, sugar, salt and a lot of canned goods. He detested canned meat and disliked canned vegetables, but he always kept enough of both to feed him if hunting was bad.

With a grateful sigh, he stowed the last of the supplies he had brought and left behind the smell of rancid burning blubber. He walked slowly around the cabin, checking the barricades of driftwood and rocks that helped to deflect polar bears and storms.

When he finished inspecting the exterior, he rolled a cigarette and leaned against a sunny cabin wall. Translucent waves whispered over the rocky beach. Cool fingers of wind riffled the turquoise sea and lifted through his dark hair. The air was rich with a clean salt smell that renewed senses dulled by cities and fatigue.

But while his body was still, his mind was busy organizing what had to be done in the next few weeks. Rocks must be gathered for the fox traps and driftwood for his fires. If he waited too long, both driftwood and stones would freeze fast to the ground. Once gathered, the driftwood must be split into kindling. Main Cabin must be repaired while the weather held. The rest of Bird Mountain's supplies must be ferried up while the weather held. And he had to hunt geese and ducks before they left. Good weather would help for that. The huskies must have food, and only a fool hunted seal from an open rowboat in bad weather. The huskies' harness must be repaired, the home-made sled must be checked for damage and all the hundred other little things must be done that combined to mean survival.

His list was thick, his time was thin. And in the remaining weeks of Arctic afternoon, he could be sure of only one thing: the weather would change quickly, often and for the worse. Past experience told him he would use the boat only in good weather, hunt geese in changing weather, collect wood and stones in bad weather and repair harness in vile weather.

From habit, he looked at the mountaintops but saw no sign of coming storms. The mountains were nearly clear of clouds. The day was almost too perfect. It could not last. Either a hard wind or a dripping fog would descend soon. He hoped it would be fog, for with fog the sea was usually calm, usually safe for a man in a small boat. Usually.

Ivar smiled at the sea, then turned away. There was work to be done.

Trills and screams and shrill calls of countless sea birds rose from Bird Mountain like mist off a lake. The racket did not wake Ivar; it was September now, late in the afternoon of the year-long Arctic day. Bird noises would be notable only if absent. But when the cloud cover broke and the sunlight changed from murky to transparent gold, Ivar stirred and awoke. His breath smoked in the cabin and he shivered when his bare feet touched the floor. He lit the fire in the converted oil drum which served as a stove. Nothing fancier was needed; the oil drum heated the 6-foot-square living area quite nicely.

Though his clammy clothes raised goose bumps all over his body, Ivar took no notice of the discomfort. He expected the cabin to be cold and damp when he woke up. He rarely was disappointed.

He moved quickly to the window and looked out. When he saw that the clouds were withdrawing, thinning, almost gone, a feeling of relief warmed his body as much as the orange fire sizzling in the makeshift stove. For eighteen days the weather had been rotten; storms preceded and followed by high winds that made the fjord impassable for days at a time, then a day or two of decent weather in which he could travel, then bad weather again. Twice he had had to turn back from seal hunting and race for the nearest cabin. He must take a seal today, or his huskies would be eating their master's food. That was a bad way to start his year.

He turned away from the mellow golden light pouring through the window and prepared a quick breakfast of oatmeal, dried fruits and strong coffee. As he ate, he looked out the window again, measuring the weather. Across the dark fjord, Hornsund Peak reflected light like a shattered diamond. A thin fall of new snow reached three quarters of the way down the mountain. The snow might melt back, but probably not. That sheer veil was the vanguard of winter. Soon the golden Arctic afternoon would slide into twilight, then night. The birds sensed the change; their calls had taken on a new urgency. The foxes knew it also; most were white already, and every day their fur thickened against the frigid night to come. And now even Hornsund Peak was trying on its own winter coat.

His mind on the coming seal hunt, Ivar hurried through his breakfast, hurried out of the cabin, hurried to where his boat was beached high on the rocky shore. He braced himself against the boat and pushed. With grating reluctance, the yellow boat moved toward the sea. The waves which had crashed head-high were today only knee-high—except for one wave, the

*View from Bird Mountain,
looking south across Hornsund Fjord.
Hornsund Peak in background*

one that curled over his right boot and soaked his foot in water that was 3 degrees removed from ice.

Cursing, he leaped into the boat. He could have beached the boat again and returned to the cabin for dry socks, but he had the not wholly irrational feeling that if he turned his back, Hornsund would whip up another storm for him. Besides, after any appreciable time in the boat, both feet would be wet and cold and, he hoped, numb.

He put his back into the rowing. If he worked hard enough, the heat from his body might warm up the water-soaked boot. If not, so be it. No one ever died of cold feet, only frozen feet.

Under his steady rowing, the boat pulled out into the fjord and around Bird Mountain peninsula. Though pressed for time, he did not tire himself; he had a long day of rowing ahead. There was too much floating ice to use the motor today. So while he was cold and wet, the machine was warm and dry in the cabin.

Out from Bird Mountain, around the peninsula, toward the closed end of Hornsund. The eastern end of the fjord was divided into two bays. Ivar called the northern bay Two Glacier Bay. The southern, Seven Glacier Bay, was larger and rimmed with 50-foot ice walls. Ringed seal were year-round residents of both bays; in fact, of all of Hornsund. They were the most numerous seal in the Svalbard Islands, and the staple of polar bears.

Ivar would prefer to take the much larger bearded seal; it represented four to six times as much blubber and flesh for the same amount of time, risk and killing as a ringed seal. Yet, like the polar bear, he would have to be satisfied with what the Arctic provided. Ringed seal were plentiful, therefore ringed seal were more likely to end up in his larder than their huge cousins.

Ivar's body moved smoothly over the oars, muscles working rhythmically. The aches and pains, heritage of a lazy summer, had been replaced by supple strength. After the long weeks of wind and sleet, it was good to be out in buttery sunlight, good to feel his body work, good to see the clouds disappear and the wind drop to a light, dry breeze.

He made fast time into Two Glacier Bay, rowing quietly, glancing over his shoulder from time to time to scan the rocks and floating ice and the two glaciers. A small peak divided the glaciers, thrusting a short peninsula out into the bay. The land was rough, but he had seen seals on the rocks before. Ice blocks, sculpted and worn by the summer sun, were also favorite hauling-out places.

Deftly, quietly, Ivar reversed his position in the boat, pushing rather than pulling on the oars. Still no seals in sight. The water, then. Perhaps the seals were not sunning today. Sometimes the hollow sound of ice chunks bumping the boat brought seals to investigate the strange, yellow-bottomed glacier calf. The curious seals approached underwater, then surfaced 20 feet away to stare with big eyes and spread whiskers at the strange upright animal who rode the wooden berg.

On other days, Ivar would enjoy the twitching whiskers and bright round eyes and easy grace of the seal. Today he was a hunter. He could not indulge his pleasure in merely watching the sleek animals. If a curious seal surfaced, he would do his best to kill it quickly and be grateful to have the hunt end successfully.

He searched each rock, each block of ice. No sleeping seals. The dark blue water held neither staring eyes nor darting forms. For all he could see, Two Glacier Bay was as devoid of seals as the moon. At the end of three hours, rowing as quietly as the squeaky left rowlock would allow, all he had for his trouble were two very cold feet and eyes that watered from staring at shiny icebergs.

For the third time, he rowed past the face of Muhlbacker Glacier at a distance of 100 yards. He would go no closer—not for all the seals in Hornsund. Flirting with calving glaciers was a sudden way to die. He stared into the small caves on the glacier's blue-green face. The ice cliff was scarred by rivulets and dirty from gravel picked up centuries ago as the ice river ground along the slopes of nameless mountains miles inland.

But both shoreline and floating ice were empty. Two Glacier had turned an icy shoulder on his hunt.

Ivar reversed his position again and rowed out of the bay, toward Seven Glacier. He rowed steadily, quietly, about 20 yards off the rugged face of Treskelen Peninsula, a thrust of rock that almost landlocked Seven Glacier Bay. He was muttering under his breath on the subject of seals when a sleek head popped out of the water no more than 30 feet behind the boat.

The ringed seal appeared so quickly that Ivar went on swearing for a moment; the fact of the seal simply did not register, even though he was looking directly at it. Then the oars stopped in midair. Slowly, slowly, he lowered the oars until they touched the water. The forward motion of the boat quietly folded the oars back beside the gunwales as he reached toward the shotgun that rested against the plank seat. He eased the protective sheath off the gun. As soon as the gun was free, his motion turned from measured stealth to lightning reflex. But the seal's reflexes were equally fast, and Ivar had farther to go. By the time the gun was to his shoulder, the seal was gone. No bubbles, no rippling trail. Just blue-black water, cold and empty.

Ivar replaced the shotgun and retrieved the waiting oars. Boredom and frustration were the hunter's enemies. He had first learned that lesson in the woods of Norway, but it was a lesson that needed to be renewed from time to time. Better to be taught by a seal than a polar bear.

The hunt had carried him halfway down the black-rock peninsula. Treskelen's sides were so sheer here that neither ice nor seal could find refuge. And even if a seal should magically appear among the slick rocks, Ivar would ignore it. There was no way to retrieve a kill from rocks he himself could not climb.

The sun was dipping toward the western arc of its daily elipse, turning the air gold. A few hours of twilight would come today, forerunner of the extended twilight of the year-long Arctic day. To Ivar, the subtle shift in light underlined the decision he had to make: turn back for Bird Mountain or continue down the peninsula, around the point, and into Seven Glacier Bay.

Swiveling the boat on its axis with the oars, he studied the weather and the wind and the light. The sky was still clear and deep, the light still that of late afternoon. Although the wind had freshened somewhat, it was still a weak wind that did little more than chop the surface water into ripples and brisk little waves. And the wind was from the northwest; it would herd most of the icebergs into the southeast corner of Seven Glacier, where the ice would be no real danger to him. His only concern would be quick-ice, peppercorn-sized knots of ice that presaged the winter freeze, in the calm waters behind the peninsula. But those same calm waters would attract seals.

Ivar weighed all the factors against his need for seal. An hour to row to the end of the peninsula, then a quick look into the bay. An hour. Not much time; he was still fresh. And in Seven Glacier, there was a good chance of taking one of the huge bearded seals. The bay was not much farther from Bird Mountain than his present position. Seven Glacier would be a good investment in time, and time was about all he had. He must take seal. If not today, then tomorrow or the next day, when the weather and the light might not be as good.

Besides, if he rowed hard enough, his feet might even get warm again.

Leaning on the oars, he set out for Seven Glacier Bay. Forty-five minutes later, he pulled twice on the right oar, turning the boat smartly. He studied the west one last time; the horizon was still a hard, crystalline blue. He reversed position in the boat and pushed once, twice on the oars. The yellow boat slid quietly past the headland as he leaned forward, hoping to catch sight of some reward for his efforts.

As he had expected, the portion of Seven Glacier in the lee of the peninsula was calm. Most of the glacier calves had been herded down into the southeast corner, where they thunked against the ravaged faces of Svalis and Menelejev glaciers. Scattered throughout the calm part of the bay were at least two dozen good-sized bergs, some trapped against rocks that protruded from the bottom of the bay, others floating with a subtle rocking motion in the quiet eddy of the tides. The seals should be there, asleep on the low-floating ice.

Fifty feet away Ivar saw a nicely rounded ringed seal sunning itself on the only accessible rock in a mile of shoreline. The seal watched him with a mixture of alarm and curiosity, ducking its head toward the water as though it were going to flee, then hesitating for a quick look at the oddly shaped intruder.

The hesitation was fatal. It gave Ivar all the time he needed to lift the shotgun and trigger one quick shot that nearly lifted the seal off its rock. As the shot echoed in the bay, he dropped the gun and rowed as fast as he could toward the rock, praying that the carcass would not slide off into deep water. He knew that the seal had died instantly, or its reflexes would have thrown it into the bay. But a dead seal has no balance and the rock was humped up in the center. It was still early for the seal to float; once in water, the carcass could sink quickly.

By the time Ivar reached the rock, the carcass had started to slip down. Hurriedly he peeled off his gloves, reached into the icy water and groped for the seal's front flippers. His shoulder muscles bunched as he pulled the carcass free and guided it around to the stern of the boat. Now to get the seal aboard.

Ivar's fingers flexed, tightening over the slippery flippers. He took several slow breaths, then began to bob the seal up and down, up and down. With each bob the seal went a little deeper, rose a bit higher as it returned to the surface of the buoyant water. He worked and waited; timing was as important as strength. Once more . . . just a little higher . . . now!

With one smooth motion, Ivar lifted 200 slippery pounds of seal over the stern, along with several gallons of achingly cold water. But he did not mind the water. The boat could be bailed, the socks and boots could be dried and the dogs could eat.

Ivar smiled, stretched the muscles in his back and arms, then began to bail.

The water in the shelter of the peninsula was very calm. In the quiet, the sun seemed to take on some of its old summer warmth. The air was almost still, and the sea lapped gently at the rocks and the edges of the small boat that rode lower now with the weight of the seal.

Ivar studied the surrounding water for telltale slicks. Even this early in fall, undisturbed water could congeal into quick-ice. In the pockets of meltwater which rode on top of the heavier salt water, quick-ice could form with amazing rapidity, congealing while he watched, coating smooth surfaces, bogging down and virtually immobilizing a small boat. He had no desire to find out how long a man could live on a rowboat in

Seven Glacier Bay, eating raw seal and hoping the rest of the sea would freeze enough to walk on before he died of exposure.

As he studied the water, he saw small slick patches where fresh water had gathered along the front of Storbreen, the closest glacier. And, on a newborn glacier calf floating near the front of the ice wall, he could just make out the black form of a big bearded seal, resting and enjoying the sun while it still had power over the cold.

That seal was safe. Ivar would have to be absolutely desperate for meat before he would hunt that close to an active glacier in autumn. His first year had taught him the price of not respecting glaciers. He had been in a hurry, taking a tempting shortcut across the sea in front of a glacier. He was nearly killed when the glacier casually dropped a 40-ton calf into the sea, raising waves that tossed his boat about like a matchstick. With every pail of water that he bailed out of his nearly submerged boat, he had promised never to be so stupid again.

Most of the time a glacier's movement was imperceptible in terms of hours or days or even months. But there were critical moments when the weight of tons of unsupported ice overcame the tensile strength of interlocked ice crystals. When that happened a hooked cornice broke off with the splintering music of an icefall, or a new calf was expelled with an immense crashing roar. The water around the berg where the bearded seal lay was choked with the debris of such falls, and slicks of quick-ice extended just beyond.

His dogs would not starve if he passed up that seal. Ivar could forget him. The risk was greater than the reward. Were any of his friends about, though? If he could take just one bearded seal, he would not have to hunt again until the sea was frozen and the glaciers were quiet and there was enough snow that the dogs could drag their own meat up to the cabin.

He turned around on the hard bench, wriggled his numb toes and resumed rowing and watching the icebergs farther out, in the relative safety of the middle bay. He rowed quietly, as quietly as the one squeaking rowlock would allow. With the vision of bearded seal haunting him, he stopped the boat. A few quick strokes of his sheath knife sliced off a chunk of ringed seal blubber. He rubbed it over the squeaky rowlock, swung the oar, rubbed again. Not perfect, but better. He wiped the knife clean and put it back in the sheath on his belt. With his back toward the main fjord, he pushed deeper into Seven Glacier Bay.

He was farther from shore now, heading quietly for a line of small bergs that seemed to have grounded on a shallow shelf a mile from the front of a glacier. The bergs were old by the standards of the bay. They had been stranded for at least one season. The summer sun had borne down on them as they rested on the shelf, smoothing their peaks and rough edges into concave and convex curves. In the hollows where ice cups focused the thin autumn sun, he hoped to find more seals.

Ivar circled 200 yards in back of the grounded bergs, approaching them from the glacier side, the shadow side, stealing quietly along, watching the ice blocks and the water around them, slipping the oars cleanly into the water, stroking, slipping them out, lifting them high to clear the small wavelets before he silently returned the oars to the sea and stroked the boat forward.

The stalk was slow, wary and tiring. Ivar did not notice his fatigue; his whole mind was fastened on the hunt.

As he neared the line of ice, he slowed his strokes and edged into a narrow space between two bergs that reached 4 to 10 feet above waterline. Shipping the oars, he let the little boat drift for a moment, then moved to the bow to look down the lateral face of the line where seals should be.

There. Two bergs down, 400 feet away. A huge bearded seal was dozing in the sun, head pointed toward the open water at the mouth of the bay.

Too far.

The bullet had to be accurate within half an inch. He had to kill the seal instantly or a massive shrug of muscles would send it deep into the sea. If he merely injured the seal, it would sink and drown and be wasted.

Ivar inched backward and picked up the oars again. With a long backward stroke he pulled the boat out of the seal's line of sight. Spinning the boat quickly, he rowed along the shadow side of the line of bergs, aiming for the back of the iceberg adjacent to the sleeping seal. In the blue shadow of the ice, he again shipped the oars and silently moved to the bow, edging carefully around the stiffening carcass of the ringed seal.

The boat rocked slightly, kept rocking even though Ivar was still. The wind was on the move. It had grown bigger teeth, and more of them, but Ivar noticed only the balance of the rifle as he freed it from its sheath. The steel barrel and the wooden stock were cold in his ungloved hands, but there was a comfortable weight to the old Mauser as he lifted it across his chest and waited for the fading momentum of the boat to carry him past the berg which hid him from the bearded seal.

The seal was still dozing, head down. The boat hesitated just behind the looming berg, blocking Ivar's aim. The boat hung for a long moment while he sat like an agonized stone. He knew that the seal could see the yellow prow, could awake and dive away before he had a chance to shoot.

Slowly, almost imperceptibly, the boat eased forward just enough to give Ivar a clear shot. The seal awoke, but it was too late; the bullet was already on its way, the rifle had already kicked against the coiled muscle of Ivar's shoulder. The big seal died even as its muscles tightened to propel it into the water. A second of alarm, a split second of shock so overwhelming as to be painless, and the seal's body stretched to its full length on the rocking ice.

Ivar slowly lowered the Mauser. As he saw that the seal would not slip off the shelf, his body relaxed. He began to breathe again. Reflexively, he slapped the bolt of the Mauser, tripping the spent cartridge from the chamber and slipping a new one up from the magazine below. He pulled the sealskin sheath back over the rifle and placed it in its spot beside the bench, opposite the shotgun.

A series of long oar strokes brought him quickly to the ice where the seal lay 3 feet above waterline. He felt a flash of regret at the shattered skullcap and the spreading red stain, then in his mind the seal became badly needed provisions and regret disappeared.

The bow of the boat nudged against the ice below the seal's hummock. Dragging the bowline in one hand and a 10-foot length of rope in the other, Ivar leaped up onto the berg. The seal was huge, more than 800 pounds. Fortunately, the carcass was lying close to the edge of the shelf. Eight hundred pounds of dead seal was an almost immovable mass. As it was, he would have to butcher it at the water's edge when he got to the cabin, for there was no snow to help him slide the heavy seal across the rocky ground. That meant more hours of cold, wet work after a long row home.

Almost unconsciously, he glanced at the sun's position, his always changing clock. It was late. Then he looked again and felt a chill move through his body. Far out beyond the peninsula, in the open waters of Hornsund, whitecaps leaped as though an invisible hand churned the sea. And behind the lines of whitecaps came the first sets of larger waves, 3 feet high now on the edge of the incoming tide, growing as he watched. He watched, time turning slowly around him, until the wind entered Seven Glacier Bay with a cold, harsh shout.

Quickly, he knelt beside the seal, whipped out the short-bladed sheath knife. He made two short slits in the seal's skin just forward of the rear flipper. Slipping the knife blade underneath the skin, he pushed through the blubber, opening a channel between the two slits. He forced the rope through the channel, then tied the rope with a slipproof knot.

Ivar leaped back down into the boat, balancing easily, and secured the other end of the rope to a bolt hole in the stern-post. Then he swung back up on the ice shelf and began pushing and shoving the seal closer to the edge of the berg. After a few minutes he was sweating freely despite the cold wind.

Easy, man, or you'll end up in the drink with the seal. Slow down and think.

Ivar straightened and took a deep breath. Then, with one last muscle-bunching heave, he tipped the balance. The seal slid over the edge of the berg and into the water. Ivar rode the rocking ice as he watched the seal sink, bob, then stabilize just beneath the surface, buoyed by the water and restrained by the line. If the wind got no worse, he could handle this 800-pound anchor.

After a quick glance around the shelf to make sure he had left nothing, he leaped into the boat and took up the oars. As he looked over his shoulder at the open water beyond the bay, his fatigue was pushed aside by his determination. He shoved off from the iceberg and rowed toward the open water off the peninsula. Time and again he had to veer off from icebergs moving across the bay and the hollow thunks of smaller ice glancing off the boat followed his progress.

Each time he looked over his shoulder, the whitecaps had moved farther down the fjord; their leaping white lines were crossing the water where he would have to make his turn for Bird Mountain. Worse, the wind was shifting and getting stronger as it rode the back of the incoming tide. Even Treskelen's bony finger no longer sheltered Seven Glacier Bay. Waves rose in the formerly calm waters. No whitecaps yet, but an occasional larger wave slapped the boat, making it wallow sluggishly. If he could have rowed directly into the waves, he would have made smoother progress, but rowing into the waves meant rowing straight into Treskelen's unforgiving cliffs. Once he was beyond the peninsula, he could turn into the waves. Breathing deeply and evenly, he put his back into rowing.

As he rowed, whitecaps moved into the bay. The wind no longer veered, but blew steady and hard from west-southwest, pushing everything down the fjord, into the bay and then against the ravaged glaciers. The bearded seal acted as a slightly buoyant anchor, dragging against the forward progress of the boat. And each wave that splashed over the gunwale added to the weight of the boat and the ringed seal inside.

Twenty minutes passed, then forty; Ivar's progress was slow but measurable. Again and again, he looked over his right shoulder toward the open fjord, watching for clouds that might mean a sleet storm or one of the frequent, unpredictable squall lines that made living in the Arctic so interesting. But the sky stayed blue and empty. His bad luck seemed confined to the west-southwest wind.

He kept the bow of the boat on a diagonal line that would take him out of the mouth of the bay 200 yards beyond the rocky headland. There was no place to land on either side of the peninsula and he wanted no part of those unyielding rocks in broken seas.

After an hour's hard rowing, he stopped to bail. He was still a quarter mile short of his goal. As he bailed, he studied the conditions he would face when he left the relative shelter in Treskelen's lee. Even here, unruly waves had left ankle-deep water in the boat, and his feet were soaked inside the rubber boots. It would be worse out there.

He bailed quickly, emptied his boots over the side and flexed his toes to make sure they were still functional. Some time ago he had lost all feeling in them.

When he turned to look at the seas he would pull into, the waves had grown—more than 3 feet now and running fast toward the ice cliffs of the seven glaciers. As he watched, the first of the ice blocks and bergs from glaciers farther up Hornsund hove into view off the tip of Treskelen, sailing majestically before the wind, so heavy that they barely rocked on the climbing waves.

Then Ivar saw the first of the real waves crash over the tip of the peninsula, shooting spray 10 feet into the air. He laid against the oars and began moving toward the turbulent gap.

The water became more and more choppy; small waves broached the gunwales time after time as he pulled away from Treskelen. He was still 80 yards short of the spot he had picked to turn into the wind when he saw the water ahead boil and buck up as though a whale had rolled over. He put both hands on the left oar and pulled, groaning, until boat and bearded seal were facing directly into the looming wave. The bow lifted slowly, lifted and kept on lifting as tons of blue-black water surged underneath the yellow keel. On top of the wave, Ivar looked anxiously over his shoulder. A diagonal heading was no longer possible; the wave had been a warning. He was closer to the headland than he cared to be, but the waves gave him no other choice.

The swell was now almost 4 feet high, with individual waves up to 5 or 6 feet and moving fast. As the boat sank into deep troughs, he lost sight of all except the dark heaving water. He had been at sea many times in a small boat, yet the loss of land always made him uneasy. At least with the bow into the wind, the boat was shipping less water. The ride would have been exhilarating, except for the fact that he was being pushed inexorably backwards into the bay, closer to the tossing icebergs that ground against towering glacier fronts.

Stroke. Stroke. Stroke. Not to make way, but to keep from losing it, and to keep the bow into the waves or be flipped like a coin. Stroke. Stroke. Stroke.

Time was meaningless, only the wind and sea and ice and the weight of the boat at the end of his straining arms were real.

The wind was at gale force now, yet the sky above was cobalt blue, untouched by clouds. The beauty of the clean sky was lost on Ivar. He had eyes only for icebergs and the black-rock peninsula which measured his progress. Each look told him he was losing way, moving backward toward the closed end of the bay, sliding closer to the flashing, floating mass of ice that broke in jagged waves across rocks and glacier fronts.

After an hour of rowing into the waves, he had been pushed more than a quarter mile down into the bay. He stepped up the rhythm of rowing for a hundred strokes and looked again at the peninsula. He was still losing way, although he had cut his rate of loss by about half. That was not good enough to keep him away from the waiting glaciers. The discovery did not surprise him. He had tried to fight gale winds before, and almost always with the same result. A man did not win against such facts of nature, he merely struggled to avoid being killed.

Ivar was trapped inside an ice-and-rock bottle whose stopper was the wind. There was no way to get ashore, no place to land if he could. The water in the lee of Treskelen offered no refuge—that area was so chopped and churned that even a duck would have to fight to stay afloat. He was better off out in the bay, where the waves at least came from one direction.

Ivar worked over the oars, long rhythmic sweeps that used every muscle in his body. Underneath the gloves and calluses new blisters puffed and grew. His shoulders and back and thighs ached their protest, but he neither slowed nor broke rhythm. Lean and pull, lean and pull.

He could cut loose his sea anchor, the dead weight of the bearded seal. The more his body ached, the more seductive the idea became. But what a waste of meat, of blubber, of effort, of the seal's life. And there was no guarantee that cutting the seal loose would ensure his own safety. Besides, the wind might shift or even die as suddenly as it had been born. If he cut loose the seal needlessly, every time he saw a seal he would remember the one he wasted because he quit too soon. The bearded seal would stay for now. He was tired and very uncomfortable, but he was not desperate yet.

Nor was he foolish. He still had a mile and a half of usable bay off the stern. After that, he would be into an icy marina filled with the grinding debris of the glacial scrapyard. He picked out a landmark, a jagged rock tooth on the side of Treskelen, a mile deeper into the bay. One mile. If he was pushed to that tooth, he would cut the rope that held the bearded seal.

Lean-pull. Lean-pull. Lean-pull.

Neither the rhythm nor the wind nor the pain varied. He could row another ten hours, easily, because he had no choice. All he had was an unbending will to survive.

Lean-PULL. Lean-PULL. Lean-PULL. Let the world shrink to a yellow boat and white ice and black waves. Time and pain had no color, no place in his shrunken world.

Wind-driven spray and breaking waves drenched him, slowly filling the boat with frigid water. He was forced to stop rowing and bail. When his numbed left hand refused to hold onto the bailing can, he wedged the can between his palms and bailed as fast as he could, stopping only to prevent the boat from sliding sideways into a wave. When he finished, he had lost a hundred yards to the tireless wind.

LEAN-PULL. LEAN-PULL. LEAN-PULL.

But at the end of two hundred wrenching strokes, he had regained less than half the lost distance. He returned to his former pace, his shrunken world, determined to hold station as long as he could. Every few strokes he checked his landmark. He was less than 300 yards above the jagged tooth and closing fast.

He looked over his shoulder, hoping to see an end to the marching whitecaps far out in the fjord. The horizon was somehow closer than he had expected. He stared intently, then realized that the sun had set while he fought the wind. There would be no real darkness, nothing more than a few hours of crimson light and shadows rising from the land. Very beautiful, if your life did not depend on judging distances accurately.

Ivar rowed, searching for a sign that the wind was diminishing with the light. What he saw was a tightly spaced flotilla of icebergs tossing into the bay. He would have to avoid them somehow, as he had avoided all the rest of the rolling ice. He needed time for that, time to see the danger, time to judge its angle of approach, time to ease the unwieldy boat with its anchor onto a safe heading. But the draining light obscured icebergs until they were dangerously close, and Treskelen's jagged tooth was gaining on him.

Ivar rowed, eyes on the closing horizon where white ice rolled.

Too close.

Not enough time.

As a red-tipped wave drenched the boat, his knife swept across the taut rope which kept the bearded seal afloat.

Good-bye, my friend. I'm sorry.

The boat lurched, bucked up, then steadied under Ivar's hands. Strength seemed to rush back into his arms; the yellow boat seemed made of air rather than wood. The sensation would pass as his muscles adjusted to pulling less than half of the former load, but he was grateful for the mental lift the relative lightness gave him. He held the yellow prow into the waves and watched the approaching bergs, automatically gauging the best course through the shining ice forest.

He could go to his left, between the peninsula and the icebergs. It was the shortest way, but he might end up smashed all over Treskelen. To his right was open water, but he would be sideways to those huge waves. That left the middle, which was like trying to sneak carrion past a polar bear.

So who said it had to be easy? Right and left are out. Grab what you can and quit bitching.

He began rowing in earnest, ignoring the water sloshing around his feet, the spray lashing across his face, the smaller pieces of ice that crunched against the boat. Normally he would have tried to miss any floating ice, but now he had eyes only for the massive bergs ahead. He strained into the red light, measuring distances and individual bergs. While he watched, several of the bergs wallowed erratically. Two of them flipped over, sending out fountains of spray and conflicting waves.

He marked the unstable icebergs; he would avoid them if he could. What he needed was big ice that would not turn turtle as he rowed by, big ice that was not too close to its neighbors.

Pulling hard on the left oar, he committed himself to a new heading, slightly off-center of the waves. He rowed quickly, lining the prow up with a gap in the two nearest icebergs. Both were big, fairly stable . . . he hoped.

At triple speed, Ivar shot through the opening, then wove

through the next obstacles. Pause, right oar, climb the wave, look, stroke, left oar, stroke, wait . . . wait . . . PULL.

Behind him, two bergs touched in grinding caress, but Ivar barely noticed. The ice off his stern was of no interest; the ice in front of him was a shining enigma he must penetrate. He looked ahead once more, measuring, calculating, then pulled the yellow boat straight into the waves with sweeping strokes of the oars.

To his left, about 40 feet off, one of the unstable icebergs bled scarlet rivulets of seawater down its flanks. He spared a fast glance for the berg's lethal beauty, then worked with redoubled energy over the oars. A small piece of ice grated down the right side of the boat; the backlash of the right oar punished his already aching hand. Automatically he renewed his grip on the oar and kept on rowing. The boat boomed and crunched through the lesser ice as he watched over his shoulder and pulled on the oars.

Before he reached the final obstacle, his neck muscles were cramped from the constant twisting strain of looking over his shoulder. He ignored the pain; if he switched positions, pushing rather than pulling on the oars, he would loose speed and maneuverability. He could not afford that, not now. There was one more narrow passage he must negotiate before he would be clear of Treskelen's reaching finger and the worst of the ice. The route to relative safety lay between one large and several smaller bergs. He could shave the big one or weave through the smaller ones. The small, nearly transparent bergs worried him. Most of them were visible only when a breaking wave limned them in foam. All of them were larger than his boat.

A triplet of big waves made Ivar's decision for him. The smaller bergs gnashed and gnawed among themselves like a pack of starving huskies. The large iceberg sailed silently on, impervious to the heaving sea.

He pulled on the right oar, veering toward the big berg. He had to pass far closer to the crenulated ice than he liked— but then, he had not liked any of this since he had cut the seal loose. He took a last sighting as the boat crested a wave, then began stroking the yellow prow through the gloaming chaos of ice. As the boat slid along the edge of the massive iceberg, he unconsciously held his breath, waiting to feel the oars wrenched from his hands or the final crunch of hull slammed against immovable ice.

When the last of the iceberg's scarred length was astern, Ivar permitted himself a tiny feeling of relief. Though there was a lot of ice left in Hornsund, the worst was behind him. He had room to maneuver again. Now all he had to worry about was his own stamina. But that, unlike the weather, had never failed him.

Ivar rowed rhythmically, endlessly. He rowed against the tide and the wind and the waves and the ice, an automaton who knew only the metronome of lean-pull, lean-pull, lean-pull. With the adrenaline gone, all that remained was hard work and determination.

As the sun lifted above the horizon, round and red and rising into gold, Ivar wearily lined up his boat just off the shore of Bird Mountain. He held the boat stationary in the surging sea, choosing the right moment for a wild rush to shore.

But getting ashore in one piece would be difficult. Between Ivar and safety, rocks combed through 6-foot breakers. The rocks he could see did not worry him too much. The ones he could not see might be lethal. Yet this was familiar land, home, and the sight of his cabin burned like fire in his numb body.

He tightened his grip on the oars, wincing at the pain of his blistered hands.

The boat rose and fell as he waited for the right wave. He needed one big enough to carry him high up the rocky beach, but not so big as to wrench the boat out of his control. He pushed back hunger and exhaustion and cold, transformed them into silent patience: he had not come this far just to wrap the boat around a rock.

Now, you son of a bitch.

He pulled hard on the oars, matching momentum with an incoming wave. In a blur of white power, the wave threw him toward the shore. At the first grate of beach meeting keel, he was over the side, bowline in hand. He staggered forward, pulling the boat up the rocky beach, using whatever help the dying wave could give him.

The last 30 feet were all his own, beyond the reach even of storm waves. Without stopping to measure his tiredness or relief, he dragged the stiff ringed seal out of the boat and up to the cabin.

The cabin was cold, damp and blessedly out of the wind. A few seconds' work over the stove brought flaring orange warmth into the tiny room. Ivar stripped off his soaking clothes and draped them near the stove. Standing close to the fire, he gulped the dregs of yesterday's coffee cut with a liberal amount of Scotch. He gnawed at a hunk of bread, then discarded it. Food could wait. What could not wait was the tapered mummy bag on the bunk.

Before the blubber melted through the coal, Ivar was inside the down bag, engulfed in sleep.

Evening

A plaintive goose call rang over Main Cabin, a single urgent honk that brought Ivar awake with a surge of adrenaline. He had been expecting to hear that call, hoping to hear it, for a week now.

The windows of the cabin glittered with heavy frost rime, and the October light was dull gray. The night had been the coldest of the season, although he had not noticed it in the goose-down bag. Now his breath smoked lazily into the room as he lay abed, snug and smug and warm. He savored the warmth; in the Arctic he had learned to live with being warm once a day, if he was lucky.

The goose called again, high and wild.

At the second call, Ivar smiled with an eagerness that answered the cry of the goose. The onset of winter excited him.

The past week had been mild and warm, as warm as 45 degrees Fahrenheit—Indian summer, Arctic style. He had used the reprieve to make final repairs on the cabins, putting the last nails in the last boards that would repel the coming blizzards. In the thinning sunlight, he had re-covered the roof of Bird Mountain Cabin with fresh tar paper, and he had renailed the siding on the west side of Main Cabin. The provision shelves at the cabins were full, and there was even seal stashed at each cabin for the dogs.

To celebrate finishing the cabins, he had taken the day off yesterday. He had played with Naika along the shore and watched the birds, laid out traplines in his mind and gathered driftwood logs, standing them on end like shocks of grain so that when the snows fell the logs would be visible above the

*View from Ptarmigan Slope above Main Cabin,
looking east up Hornsund Fjord*

drifts instead of buried and frozen to the ground. Handling the cold logs was not work to him; it was an excuse for a little walking, a little thinking and a lot of enjoying what might well be the last warm hours of the Arctic day.

Winter was preparing to lay siege to Hornsund; he had felt it in the wind, underneath the warmth, waiting. And so had the geese, restless on burnished tundra plains.

A third call, urgent, haunting, swept over the cabin. Whatever natural clock mapped geese days and weeks and cycles had sounded its alarm. The call was picked up by another goose, then another and another.

Migration had begun, and now he had only two days in which to stock his own larder with geese. He wriggled out of the bag and dressed quickly. While his coffee and oatmeal cooked, he stood in the doorway of the cabin, looking toward the gray sea. Naika crawled out from under the bed to join him, cold nose against warm hand. He squatted next to her, murmuring softly and rubbing her thick fur.

Somewhere behind the mist the sun shone, fighting to burn through. It would be a losing battle. Hornsund's thick mists would not yield except fleetingly, about noon, halfway through the seven hours of sunlight. But through the mist flew ghostly gray-brown shadows, leaders of the migration of the Spitsbergen geese. Singly and in pairs and triplets, the geese were gathering into flocks.

Naika whined and moved restlessly, wanting to run after the low-flying birds, but he ruffled her fur and told her to stay; he wanted to savor the sounds and sights of migration for a moment.

How I envy the geese! When they feel the urge, they go. No bags or cartons, no ships and rule books and waiting, noth-

*ing but themselves . . . and the hunters. Hunters by the thou-
sands, with twelve-gauge shotguns like mine.*

*But all the same, I envy the geese. The risk would be well
worth the freedom . . . the freedom and the flight.*

And far above him, invisible, he heard the cold, thin call
of skeins from farther north, passing overhead at 1,000 or 2,000
feet, calling up their kind from the tundra and from the small
rocky islets out at sea.

The mists swirled a little in the morning wind, then
parted, making a corridor to the sea. In the opening he saw
more fleeting shapes, geese flying low, wings working as the
birds began climbing to migration altitude. He watched the
geese passing, dark against the gray mist, and listened to their
hypnotic calling.

But as the birds had their imperative, he had his; winter
would be long and hungry if he did not take geese. He motioned Naika back and reached for the shotgun that rested just
inside the doorway. He would shoot from where he stood,
melting with the mist and shadow into a single dark form of
man and cabin.

When he broke open the gun, the brass cartridge bases
flared in the light, both primers undimpled. He snapped the
weapon shut; the breech and primed barrels made a metallic
clink.

From the mists to his right, off in the direction of Fox
Valley to the northwest, he heard a sharp call unanswered,
then another sharp call, again unanswered. He raised the gun
across his chest, waiting and watching, gauging the speed and
guessing when the bird would flash momentarily into the tunnel through the fog.

There. Now.

The goose materialized flying low and fast, wings beating

Autumn fog. Boat on right side is used for very heavy ice. Fiberglass boat on left is used for normal ice.

rhythmically, head turning left and right in quick movements as though it sought its now vanished friends. The shotgun traveled to Ivar's shoulder as though on a track. The barrels swung left, leading the goose by a yard and a half. But the wavering misty light deceived Ivar. As the sound of the shot echoed away over the sea, he heard the *flap-flap-flap* of the thoroughly frightened goose as it fled down the coast.

Damn! Fifteen cents and no goose. Oh, well, at least it was a clean miss.

Not the best way to start a day's hunting, but he had the second barrel charged—and he had the measure of the mist. The geese were farther away than they seemed in the narrow opening between fog curtains. He waited, shotgun raised and aimed at the point where a goose probably would appear.

Another honk, impatient this time, again to the right, in the swirling misty depths. Ready.

In the split second in which the bird burst out of the mist, Ivar noted that its feet were richly pink, the body relatively small, the wing beats very rapid—a young bird, unmated. The shot spread through the fog and the goose flew into an invisible wall, crumpling and somersaulting in midair, flopping to the ground like a feathered sack. A good shot, clean and quick.

He broke the weapon and the two spent shells snapped out and over his shoulder. Reaching back inside the open door, he grabbed four more shells from the box on the ledge and fed two of them into the empty chambers.

A honk, an answering honk, a pair close together, a little higher this time. The gun came to his shoulder and the pair flashed into view, one just above the other, 15 feet above the ground and 40 yards away. Bright feet and small bodies, wings working hard. He triggered two shots almost simultaneously, and the Spitsbergen geese fell together as they had flown.

He broke the shotgun again and reloaded it before he and Naika went out to retrieve the geese. As they walked, two more geese appeared silently, barely 6 feet off the ground. He was aware only of the feathery whisper of wings, then of two shapes flaring out to either side as Naika leaped up, teeth shining as she tried to drag down a meal. But the mist swallowed the geese up as quickly as they had appeared, and from down the shoreline he heard one goose call to the other as if to verify that each had seen the mist grow sudden teeth.

Ivar collected the three dead geese with a feeling of satisfaction. All three were indeed young; this was probably their first migration. With the shotgun over his shoulder and geese in hand, he headed back for the cabin. Naika sniffed longingly, but otherwise ignored the geese. The birds swung loosely, pink feet flashing. Though young, the geese made easily 18 pounds, a healthy heft, a good morning's bag for a pleasure hunter. But for a man preparing against a long winter and snow-buried spring, the geese were neither enough nor pleasure.

When the geese were safely hung by their heads from wire loops in the storeroom, he thought again of breakfast. The geese would cool quickly in the damp cold air, and if winter were as close as he suspected, he would have no worries about spoilage.

Inside the living room of the cabin, the fire had made headway against the chill, and the coffeepot was wreathed in fragrance. He prepared his meal quickly and ate it without relish. Today would be a long day, and tomorrow too. After that, the geese would be gone; the migration began one day and ended the next. From that time until the melt, it would be as though Hornsund had never heard of geese.

When he returned to the doorway, the wind blew with more strength. The mist shifted and rose, unveiling the landscape for 300 yards down the Hornsund coast, gathering around the high slopes and mountain peaks, and the sea shone oily gray. Naika whined and waved her tail hopefully, but Ivar knew the long day's hunt was not for her. He slung his pack-sack over one shoulder and the shotgun over his other and motioned Naika to stay. As he passed the doorway, he remembered the way his first shot had gone; he added a second box of shells to the packsack. They bumped heavily on his rump as he headed up the shoreline toward the Fox River delta.

Above him, hidden by the fog, he heard the hurried gabbling of passing flocks as they moved off across Hornsund, headed toward their last landfall at the south end of Spitsbergen and then out over the ocean toward the northern tip of Norway. Most of the flocks were high, but their distant voices enlivened the fog and gray light.

The morning cold had lifted a little by the time he came to the flatlands below Fox Valley. Here a group of boulders formed a small natural blind from which he could watch both the water and the inland flyway. The rock shadows allowed him to raise the shotgun without spooking the geese; their eyes were their best protection, and little movement escaped them.

He settled into the damp, cramped blind, his loaded shotgun cradled in his left arm, and waited.

A sound from the left caught his attention. A pair of King eiders came winging in low over the lapping waves and then pulled up a few feet as they crossed the seashore. Their wings beat quickly as they hurried along. They flashed past his rock blind almost close enough to touch with the shotgun barrel. In the last few feet, the eiders spotted him and flared away wildly, one sailing high and the other dropping low. Their instincts for self-preservation were perfectly in tune. Had he tried to take them, he would have faced a split-second choice, high or low, and hunting was a matter of split seconds. Today he only watched the ducks. Next week he would take a few to add variety to his winter's diet.

For many minutes, long minutes, he stood silently, moving only his eyes, watching the inland flyway and the water in turn. Through the overhanging mist he could still hear passing flocks, but they were all far too high. He felt an instant's unease . . . what if all the geese had fled? He needed their rich meat to sustain his body, needed to see their plump shapes in cold storage and know that hunger would not be an unwelcome companion through the coming months. The flocks were so huge, his needs so little by comparison. Surely the land would not withhold food from a hunter who did not waste its creatures.

Then, in answer to the food hunter's prayer, five fat Spitsbergen geese dropped down through the overcast, 40 yards off, flying perhaps 30 feet above the ground, heading for the tundra and one last feed before the long flight.

They never saw Ivar as he quietly lifted the gun to his shoulder and cracked off both barrels, dropping the third and fourth bird. The kills were quick; the geese folded and dropped to the mossy ground and lay in the perfect stillness of death. The remaining birds lifted frantically into the fog.

He hiked out to pick up the geese and returned them to the blind, placing them to one side, behind the rocks. He reloaded the gun and settled back to waiting and watching both flyways.

The next bird was a single on the inland side, a cautious goose flying alone and weaving and bobbing as though it sensed danger. Ivar watched as the bird winged into sight close to the ground. With a single fluid movement, Ivar swung out of the shadows.

The goose was quick. As it saw him, it dropped a foot and then rose sharply, veering off the left and climbing away toward the rocky slope that rose from the shoreline. The flight cut the angle of the shot; the goose was heading dead away at 50 yards when Ivar brought the gun to bear. He passed the target and let the solitary goose fly on, although the shot would not have been difficult. No sense in filling a goose so full of shot that he would have to chew each mouthful carefully, hunting for the tiny lead pellets. It was early; he could afford to go for the side shots, put the pattern out in front of the bird. If he went for the easy body target, someday he would split a tooth on lead shot.

The goose sped on, frightened by the encounter but otherwise unharmed. Ivar lowered the shotgun and moved back into the cramped blind to wait—and shiver in the numbing chill.

It was at times like this that he had difficulty understanding people who hunted solely for pleasure. For him, the most pleasant part of hunting was the knowledge that the geese would feed him, and the hope that the fox and bear pelts he took would bring enough money to buy another year of Arctic life. He killed what he must and was grateful for what the land provided.

Yet he had met people who drew back in distaste when they discovered that he hunted for his living. These people assumed that because someone else killed their food, they were morally superior to him. The first few times he encountered that attitude he became very angry. Later he ignored it and finally learned to laugh at it.

The Arctic had taught him to be patient and to cherish

life. It had also taught him an old, forgotten truth: life eats, and killing is part of the meal.

The waiting lengthened, then ended as five birds appeared over the water, closing quickly with the land, gliding purposefully toward the tundra. He watched them pull up as they crossed the shoreline. They passed in front of him, flying more slowly now, heads turning to one side and the other as they surveyed the feeding lands below. The last two geese were smaller, feet bright and pink with youth, flying side by side, very close together. Ivar snapped the gun to his shoulder and tripped off one shot, throwing a pattern of shot wide enough to take both birds. They fell swiftly, silently.

The sound of his shot scattered the three remaining birds. He picked the smallest of the three and dropped it with a single shot as it broke in front and tried to double back to the sea.

He had barely reloaded when another pair of geese appeared higher up, but well within range. The shotgun came up smoothly, tracked, then stopped. The geese were large, feet a pale grayish pink, adults. Probably mates. His chances of getting both geese were minimal. These geese paired for life; he had no wish to hear the tremulous, piercing cries of a goose calling to its dead mate.

For the next six hours he shot, retrieved, loaded and waited, taking seventeen geese while light remained in the brief autumn day. All around him he saw birds on the wing, gathering in larger and larger flocks, some of them passing just out of range to settle on the flatlands east of the peninsula, others settling onto the choppy waters to gabble among themselves, resting for the long flight that lay ahead.

And high above the resting geese, countless skeins crossed the sky. Already thousands of geese had passed, and now thousands more were riding the ice-tipped winds as he watched and listened with increasing wonder.

What mechanism did they obey, what pulled them into the cold winds and kept them there in formations that had their own natural geometry? Wedges that flared out from a single point into a widening fan, a hundred geese flying as one, hour after hour. How did they choose their leaders, how did they maintain their intervals, except by common agreement? There was a fascinating natural logic to their lives. Men could learn from that logic, that agreement on goals and destinations.

The light was fading into early afternoon dusk. He glanced at the pile of geese beside him in the blind; three more would fill his self-imposed limit of twenty. One way or another he could lug twenty back to the cabin in a single trip. Any more would be a real problem. He might have to make an extra round trip, 2 miles each way, a prospect he did not enjoy. Worse, however, was the risk of leaving a cache of geese unguarded—prey to the hungry mercies of the foxes and scavenger birds that hunted for just such windfalls.

The mist was sliding back down the mountainsides; soon he would have to head back to the cabin. He shifted position, easing his weight from cramped muscles to muscles that were merely numb. His shoulder ached from the sharp recoils. It would be worse tomorrow, when he hunted again for the rest of the geese he needed for the winter. But with forty geese, and a few ducks, he could put up the shotgun for the season.

As he watched the misty ceiling drop to 50 feet or less, he decided to quit for the day. Then a small flock of geese popped out of the fog and set their wings, dropping toward the little knoll to his left. Ten birds. Unless they veered, he should get at least two of them. He waited motionlessly, tracking the geese with his eyes. Dying light and descending tendrils of mist wavered over the birds, blurring details into formless gray. On an unseen signal, the geese banked toward the sea, passing in front of him at 30 yards. Their plump breasts caught the fading light as he threw the gun to his shoulder, tracking the leader, tripping the shot, and then drawing another bead as the first bird fell. The second shot was too low. The goose he had selected flared in alarm at the instant he fired. Most of the pellets passed just below it, but not all.

He watched the injured goose fall slowly. It called once, short and strained, then it hit the rocky ground with enough force to break its graceful neck. His relief evaporated as his eyes remembered its twisting fall: the feet had been more gray than pink. He could only hope that it was less than three years old, not yet mated.

A single, searching call destroyed that hope.

He swore as he listened to the haunting echoes of the second goose calling for its fallen mate. The other geese had fled, leaving only the one whose cries faded in and out of the mist. Ivar leaned forward slightly, straining to see into the gloom. He knew the bird would circle back, seeking its mate . . . there, a dark shadow arcing out of the fog, too far away; wait and listen to those lonely calls.

The gander cried again, seeking, pausing, crying again and pausing for the response that would never come. Ivar knew that the gander could see the two fallen geese 20 yards in front of the blind. He stayed very still, hoping the gander would come in closer. Unless the gander returned, Ivar would be haunted by those calls for as long as there was light for the gander to see his mate. Eventually, he would be driven south by the cold and lack of food. But even if he should manage to find his flock again, he would not mate; he would be nothing but a bachelor outcast, useless to his species.

So Ivar waited, barely breathing, as the calling gander

hung out in a large circle, sailing 200 yards away and always watching. Then the gander began to tighten the circle, silent now. Closer and closer, 150 yards, then 120.

As the gander came nearer, Ivar saw that he was large and strong. A nearly spent shot would not be good enough. The gander would have to be within 60 yards. Fifty would be better. But the old gander showed no desire to come that close. Ivar, moving only his eyes, checked the horizon. The light was almost gone.

Hurry, my sad friend.

The gander climbed again, then banked suddenly, lining up for a pass right over his mate, just below the ceiling of mist. As the gander approached, Ivar held his breath, then flowed out of the blind, raised the gun and fired both barrels. Sixty-five yards, a long but not a hopeless shot. The gander met the charge and died in midair, wings set in a hard line. A long descent brought the bird down more than 100 yards away.

Ivar lowered the shotgun, grateful for an evening no longer rent by the living searching for the dead. He broke the shotgun methodically and extracted the spent shells, dropped bright new ones into the chambers and closed the gun with a tired snap. He sighed and automatically gathered up the spent shells that littered the ground at his feet, stowing the shell casings in the bottom of his packsack.

He stuffed geese into the sack methodically, filling it to the top with eight before running out of room. He tied the rest of the geese in bundles with a loop around each neck. When all but three of the geese were ready to carry, he laid the bundles aside and straightened up to gather the last geese. As he stepped out of the blind, he thought he saw one of the dead birds move—the old gander, which was farthest from the blind.

Ivar made a sound of disbelief and peered into the dusky

light. The gander was moving, but not on his own. He was being towed across the tundra by a fox.

The fox had already shed most of its summer coat, and the white winter fur gave it the illusion of being as large as its windfall meal. But Ivar could see from the fox's jerky progress that the goose outweighed it by a good deal.

The fox had the gander's head in its mouth. The long flaccid neck allowed the bird's body to trail back squarely between the fox's legs, tripping the thief every second or third step.

The fox had made 80 yards while Ivar worked in the blind and was almost 200 yards away. He shouted, but either the fox did not hear or was not about to give up the gander. Ivar shouted again and saw that it was no use. If he wanted the gander, he was going to have to go and get him. Shouldering the shotgun, he set off at a fast trot.

The fox chose that moment to stop and blow, and spotted Ivar immediately. Fox studied human for an instant, measuring the distance. Finding the risk acceptable, the fox grabbed a new purchase on the gander's neck and took off again, this time dragging the booty to one side and half galloping, every muscle straining.

Ivar quickly discovered that a trot would not get the job done. The fox was still holding ground, galloping in spite of the gander's bumping and thumping alongside, and the talus slope was getting closer. If the fox was the young vixen that he had spotted a month ago, her den was close, and he might easily be out one fat bird.

He picked up the pace, closing the gap to 75 yards, and shouted again. The fox bolted, still holding onto the gander.

For an instant, Ivar considered the shotgun on his shoulder, but decided that was too harsh a penalty for petty theft. Particularly when the thief was as brave as she was beautiful.

With a burst of speed, he gained 15 yards on the vixen and yelled loudly. The fox leaped forward, losing her grip on the gander for an instant. But she was game; she stopped long enough to grab the bird's head again and raced off with renewed determination.

Ivar began to feel silly, but he was damned if he would let the little vixen get away. He had worked too hard for that particular bird.

The vixen was 50 yards from the talus slope now, and he was 30 yards behind her. He had been running hard, and feeling it, but he took up a toneless cry, noise without words, just to let the vixen know how close he was.

The fox neither looked back nor yielded her catch despite the yelling, puffing, pounding monster right on her heels. But her tail was sinking now, and her pace was labored. She was almost spent. Finally, 30 yards from the entrance to her den, the vixen slowed. Ivar closed to 10 yards and swooped down in midstride for a rock, which he pegged over the fleeing fox. The rock landed a few feet in front of her, startling her so much that she let go of the gander and shied to one side, then veered back toward her den at top speed.

Puffing and panting, Ivar trotted to where the dead gander lay. He swore at the vixen, hiding just inside her den as if to show she was not afraid after all. Vixen and hunter exchanged glares for a moment, and he suddenly realized just how angry he was. But as soon as he admitted it, he knew that his anger stemmed from a wounded, mated goose, not a thieving fox. He stepped back one pace and relaxed. After a cramped day in a cold blind, he had to admit that it was good to run and sweat a little.

He laughed aloud, startling the fox.

Still smiling, he knelt beside the big gander. Beneath the heavy feathers the bird was still warm. Ivar studied him for a moment, then reached beneath his parka and lifted the sheath knife from its scabbard. With sure strokes, he cleaned the bird, flipping the entrails onto the ground where they steamed in the cold air.

The vixen's jet-black nose poked out of the den, twitching at the scent of food lying so close.

Yes, little thief, it's yours. You earned it. But don't try it again.

As Ivar plodded back over the tundra, the fox crept out of her den. She flowed over to the unexpected bounty, but had eyes only for the retreating hunter. Then, with incredible speed, she snatched the closest piece of food and disappeared back into her den. When no shouts came, she emerged again, waited, watched, then trotted forward and began eating with ravenous delicacy.

It was a fine, crystalline November day, with an icy edge to the wind. Long, thin clouds glowed gold and scarlet, like satin streamers flying above velvet shadow mountains. In six hours the colors would drain into blue and ebony and the silver of a rising moon. Six hours . . . so little light out of twenty-four, yet the light had such beauty that Ivar would not have traded those short hours for twelve of normal sunshine.

He climbed quietly, letting the colors wash over him. From his position high on Ptarmigan Slope behind Main Cabin, he saw nothing moving, no life except his own breath curling up to the flaming sky.

He shifted the .22 rifle and rolled himself a cigarette. It was Sunday, a day of rest, but not out of any religious necessity. There simply was nothing else to do. The geese were taken, and the ducks; the traps were ready for the opening of fox season, and the driftwood stood like shocks of grain down the coast, waiting for consignment into cabin fires. He had one last task before winter, ice fishing, but Fox Lake, 4 miles west of Main Cabin in a canyon slanting back from the sea, was not yet frozen. So it had seemed a perfect time to hike up the mountain, and if he encountered the first ptarmigan of the winter, so be it; his fox traps needed bait, and his mouth watered at the thought of roast ptarmigan.

A small storm had moved through Friday, one day after he had finished his goose hunting, and swept the remainder of the summer birds out of Hornsund. The dovekies, sensing the shift in the weather, had fled all of an afternoon, shrieking their farewells into the wind. Now Hornsund would be quiet for six months, except for the wind and ice. He missed the little dovekies, but not too much. Their frenetic lives made the fjord ring with sound, but it had begun to wear—the incessant racket day and night, night and day. After they had gone, he found the silence not at all oppressive. In the Arctic twilight, his life and the hidden lives around him were being stripped to their essentials.

The climb up the slope was slow; the rocks were slick with snow and ice. He had to be very careful of his footing and handholds as he hauled himself up the face of the slope. But it was more than worth the trouble.

In this place I am complete. I know why I'm here, rather than in a city full of people and parties and colored lights. I don't always like myself as I am with other people. There's something unnatural about the way I must control and weigh and study my responses. They expect certain things of me— son, friend, lover, enemy, brother, citizen, soldier, what have you. Those things are nothing here.

I'm not a god here. I can't make the wind blow or the snow fall. Sometimes I can't even make my huskies behave. But I'm the next thing to a god. I'm a man, alive, and no thanks to anyone else for it.

He climbed to the ridge that topped Ptarmigan Slope and ran off laterally to the east. He rested there, with the knife edge of the ridge pressing cold against his buttocks, and surveyed the rocks that tumbled away from his feet to the flatlands that supported Main Cabin. The waters of the small bay at the front of the cabin were filling with chips and chunks of ice, remnants of bergs and glacial icefalls that had been swept out of the end of Hornsund by an unusual east wind. It was a landscape of rich browns and glistening white and the deep blue-black of the fjord's waters. Obsidian, bottomless and cold.

To his left was a 40-foot-wide gravel chute, covered now with a thin sheet of autumn ice. The chute stretched from the ridge top into the slope and terminated in a cluster of large boulders. His eyes measured the length of the slide and he shook his head ruefully, remembering that first year. He had been lucky then, very lucky.

He had been hunting the first ptarmigan of the season, and had shot one on the other side of the slide. The bird was not far away, 40 feet at most. He could have and should have gone back down the slope and climbed up on the opposite side of the chute. But he started across, though he knew the footing would be tricky.

He was half right. Tricky for the first 20 feet, then impossible. He slipped, twisted, fell heavily on his back and began to slide headfirst down the slope like a one-man toboggan without the toboggan.

The ice-covered chute was perhaps 400 feet long, straight down the steep slope; his nylon wind suit did nothing to slow him. At that point he was unhurt, but the fact gave no comfort as he whizzed downwards. People are not killed by falling—landing is where the trouble comes. His only chance was to turn himself around, to hit the rocks with his boots rather than his head. But turning around would be difficult, for he was moving so fast that the land blurred before his eyes.

As the slide flattened out slightly, making its last run toward the boulders, he had dug in with his left heel and hand. Slowly, slowly, his body pivoted, until with a last desperate scramble he brought his feet around to meet the rocks.

He remembered wondering if Fredrik would find him. Ivar had already given his partner a lot of grief, and now he had almost begun to hope that the fall would finish him, because if it did not, Fredrik surely would. Ivar had taken an unnecessary chance—to Fredrik any chance was unnecessary—and had lost the gamble. Now Ivar would pay the price.

He remembered the end of that slide very well. He had hit a big rock with his boots, *whango,* and the shock had numbed his feet. The impact pitched him upright and then over the rock, bruising shins, knees, chest and forehead.

The first sensation was of nothing except shock, and as he slid headfirst down the far side of the rock, he could not tell what, if anything, was broken. Then the pain came, a good sign. If you hurt, you were still alive. He tried to lever himself upright, groaning.

He tried moving his legs, but they seemed to belong to someone else. And the way they felt, that someone was welcome to them. Finally he peeled himself off the ground and leaned against the boulder, breathing slowly and hurting all over. After a few more minutes, he began to pick his way down to the cabin, nearly a mile away. Most of the trip was spent in teaching himself to walk. By the time he reached the cabin, he was doing a reasonable imitation of a man who had been walking for nineteen years.

The last thing he needed then was another lecture from Fredrik. He had already been chewed out too many times for taking unnecessary chances. And he did not feel good enough to argue the semantics of "unnecessary" with Fredrik. Ivar decided not to tell him.

But now, four years later, Ivar still wondered if Fredrik had not guessed that something had happened. Even though Ivar's clothes had not ripped on the rockslide, he must have looked awful. But Ivar said nothing, and Fredrik did not ask. Perhaps he was as tired of yelling as Ivar was of being yelled at. And some things were just easier not to know. . . .

After another few minutes on the knife edge of the ridge, Ivar stood and stretched a little in the wind, watching the last golden bolts of sun burnish the tips of the eastern mountains. Then, gancing around the nearby rocks for ptarmigan and finding none, he retraced his lateral path back down the slope, moving carefully.

Two days later, the weather was still cold and clear as Ivar skied through midmorning twilight toward Fox Valley. He carried a hand ax, and the frames of two fox traps were strapped to the packboard on his back. Naika romped alongside, kicking snow dust over his skis. He was pushing the ski season, but with luck, he would not have to carry the cross-country skis over more than two bare stretches. As he approached Fox River's sea outlet, he scanned the land carefully. Yesterday, on his way to set out the gill net beneath Fox Lake's new ice, he had spotted two more possible trap sites, small rocky knolls which the wind would keep free of snow. Today he would lay out the traps.

Naika did not share his working mood. She danced like a pup around him, chasing off toward heaps of rock and after shadows and anything else which offered the slightest excuse for a snow-plowing dash. Ptarmigan hollows and fox trails and the rest of the world of smells tormented and delighted her;

she doubled and tripled the distance he covered as she pursued elusive scents in the twilight land.

The temperature had dropped to zero, but the air was still. Ivar's and Naika's breath hung in front of them, drifting and finally dissipating into the thin, dry air.

When he approached the little peninsula which he had selected for one of the traps, he called to Naika, warning her to stay. One foreign scent at a trap site was unavoidable, but two were. The shy and crafty foxes would not venture onto the peninsula if Naika's scent were present.

Naika was used to the routine; she took the command to heart, sitting on her brown haunches, ears up and eyes alert as Ivar moved the 100 yards out onto the peninsula. Her whole posture declared that she would faithfully wait on this appointed spot until the moment his voice released her. And it could be no other way, or he would have left her at the cabin. As much as he enjoyed Naika's company, the business of trapping was too important to be spoiled by an ill-trained pet.

He surveyed the little tip of the peninsula for the best trap site, trying to guess how more snow would change the contours of the ground. Dropping the ax, he stripped off the pack and freed one of the traps.

The trap was simple, a 30-inch-square lattice of sawed lumber. He laid the trap flat on the chosen site and scouted around for conveniently sized rocks to put on top of the boards. He would not set the trap yet, though fox season had officially begun. He would wait two more weeks and be absolutely sure that whatever fox died in his traps would be wearing the full depth of its silky winter fur. If the fox were still in transition fur, the pelt would be worthless.

After his own fox season began, he would return to the traps, tip the square up on end, then complete the trap by

Fox trap

adding a simple device Fredrik had taught him to make—a trigger stick that locked the two prop sticks together just tightly enough to support the trap and the 80 pounds of rock that would be piled on top of it. The bait, a ptarmigan head, was attached to the trigger. If that stick moved, the trap collapsed.

The weighted lattice would be poised on top of the trigger in such a way that a fox could not grab the bait unless the fox stood underneath the frame. Few foxes were quick enough to take the bait and avoid the falling trap. His traps had no middle ground: if the fox was trapped, it died instantly; if not, the fox was unscathed. No metal teeth grinding into a leg, driving its victim to a frenzy that ended in exhaustion and slow freezing death, or driving the fox to gnaw off its own leg and then face an even slower death by starvation or gangrene.

Close to the spot that he had chosen he saw a pile of rocks, shore stones and small boulders of exactly the type he needed. Had he not been intent on readying the trap, he might have wondered at his luck, but he moved toward the convenient collection without hesitation. The land provided so sparingly that he had long ago learned not to question its small concessions.

The rocks were scattered, but still retained a ragged oval shape 5 feet long and 3 feet wide. At the edges of the pile were irregular smaller stones; the rocks toward the middle were the size of melons. He picked up several of the larger ones and cradled them in one arm while he reached for more. As he lifted the fifth rock, he uncovered a grayish white curve of bone. Gently he lifted a sixth stone, and gray curves became a smooth convex surface. The bone had once protected a man's brain, the blank hollows had once been eyes.

Carefully, he put the rocks he was holding aside and lifted

*One of many unmarked graves
along Hornsund's coast*

several more away from the skull, shocked and yet intrigued. In silence he studied the skull and the bone fragments that had once anchored shoulder and chest muscles. The rib cage had sagged under the weight of time, but each portion of the skeleton could be identified.

He studied the skeleton for a long moment, seeking any sign that might explain the enigmatic grave. He had heard stories of whalers from the seventeenth and eighteenth centuries dying of scurvy or hunger or fear of months without light. Some of the men had been buried on desolate Svalbard shores, hundreds of miles from their homes in Thalwalkie or Odessa or Portsmouth or Hammerfest. It had been a teeming land then, rich with countless walrus and whales. But the whalers and hunters had pursued their prey—and themselves—into extinction.

He rolled one of the rocks from hand to hand, watching the muted play of light along its rough surface. The rock looked no different from a thousand other rocks he had held, yet it had protected the remains of a man against storms and scavengers for unknown years. His eyes moved to the skull, weathered and gray, far less durable than the rock. The passage of time had ground the skull's edges down and cracked its high places.

At least he was not alone. Someone piled these rocks over his grave. That's more than I might expect.

But then, I am not going to die.

Gently, he replaced the rocks that shielded the skull. He straightened the smaller rocks that had formed the border of the grave, then quietly stood upright. He gathered his tools and traps and left without looking back.

As he hiked up the peninsula, he remembered Naika sitting patiently on the mainland. He called to her and there was an explosion of snow as she ran to meet him. He did not wave her off, for he no longer cared that the peninsula would be contaminated by her scent. There were other, better places to trap. He propped the traps against a particularly high pile of rocks to be collected on his way back from the lake.

As the short hours of light swelled to noon, Ivar and Naika climbed up the rocky route into Fox Valley. Just one crimson edge of the sun reached above the horizon. He stopped for a moment, savoring the red-gold light, storing it in body and mind against the long winter night. The anticipation of sunless months lay on his mind more heavily than any other aspect of Arctic winter. Cold could be combated or endured, as necessary. Darkness was another matter . . . somehow a kerosene lamp seemed less adequate against the polar night than a small wood fire against the polar cold.

He resumed the climb up into the valley, where Fox Lake lay rigid beneath ice and shadow, surrounded by peaks blazing scarlet and gold. The icy lid that capped Fox Lake was blue-black beneath mountain shadows; a band of wind-driven snow gleamed white along one side of the lake. For now, most of the ice was clear. Later, the lake would be totally buried under yards of snow, for Fox Lake was in the lee of the mountains, where snow piled deepest.

He hiked across the rocky approach and down to the ice. Naika ranged ahead, tail waving eagerly as she made for the smooth center. The frozen lake was both playground and nemesis for the big shepherd. Ivar watched her, smiling.

Head high, nose testing the wind, Naika trotted 50 yards out onto the ice. Then she paused and began angling back toward shore. Her speed increased as she approached a small cove where the jumbled rocks of a talus slope fell down to the margin of the lake.

He could tell that Naika was on a scent of some sort, but

Ice fishing on Fox Lake

he did not call her off. If it were fox, fine. If it were bear, he should know.

When Naika was 100 feet from shore, a small white shadow flashed out across the cove ice, heading for the shelter of the talus slope. The effect on Naika was electrifying—she sprang forward with every bit of strength in her large brown body.

But the ice defeated her from the first bound. Her claws were useless on the hard, smooth surface. She loooked like a squirrel on a treadmill, making only inches of headway for all her churning efforts. The fox had better footing. The cove was covered with snow, providing a perfect surface for the fox's light-footed lightning run. And the fox knew it. A quick shift of direction brought the fox obliquely toward the shore, forcing Naika to veer in order to follow. She tried—and ended up pitching forward on the point of her chin, sprawling and skidding across the slick ice.

Ivar took pity on her and stifled his laughter long enough to call to her, giving her a graceful exit from the uneven contest. As the white fox disappeared into the talus slope, Naika cautiously regained her feet. When she was satisfied that her legs would obey, she turned toward Ivar and trotted back, tail waving and pink tongue tossing. She waited patiently while he removed his skis, stood them upright in the snow and walked carefully onto the ice.

The day before, he had chopped a series of holes through the 4-inch thickness of ice. Strung between the holes was a 100-foot gill net. The straight line of holes cut across the current flowing out of the lake into the river. He had no difficulty in finding his holes again; the chunks he had chipped out still littered the area, the only imperfection on the blue-black floor of ice.

Naika took the lead again, more gingerly this time but still eager. Those ice chips were among her favorite playthings.

By the time he reached the first hole, Naika had finished inspecting it. The frozen-over hole offered no play for her, so she seized a fist-sized chunk of ice, lay down and gnawed on it like a bone. The ice could have had no more attraction for her if it were a reindeer haunch.

Ivar set to work reopening the first ice hole with his ax. As the ring of steel on ice echoed in the still air, Naika abandoned her prize and trotted over to inspect the hole again. This time there was a patch of open water just big enough for her to get paw and nose into. She lapped loudly, then nuzzled his face, dripping ice water all over him.

He sputtered and shoved her away, sending her skidding 10 feet across the ice. She returned immediately, eyes alive with play as she poised herself for another slide. It was a game both had enjoyed many times. He pretended to ignore Naika as he worked at widening the ice hole. Naika oozed closer, waiting for an opening. If she could flatten him on the ice, the best game of all would begin—wrestling. But as she gathered herself for the leap, his hand flashed out and sent her spinning and sliding across the ice.

Ivar's laughter was answered with a throaty yap. Naika closed in again, tail waving eagerly. He knew this game of stalk and slide could last as long as he had strength to play. But the net must be tended, and light was limited. He scooped up a newly chopped chunk of ice, showed it to Naika and then skated it across the ice. She leaped after the whizzing chunk and followed it almost to the middle of the lake.

By the time she returned, prize in mouth, he had opened the first and last hole in the line and had loosened the far end of the rope. Naika dropped the ice and moved aside, knowing that play was over for now. Ivar stripped off his gloves and began pulling the net out of the water. Though the frigid cords made his hands ache, being bare-handed was better than facing the long hike home with soaked and frozen gloves.

He had pulled no more than 5 feet of net when the first fish hung up on the edge of the hole. A 6-pound Arctic charr, a salmonlike fish he had come to prize as a break from his diet of birds. The fish was tangled in the cords and as rigid as stone. In the icy black water, a fish that could not swim was very quickly frozen.

The charr had entered the lake from Fox River sometime earlier in the season, probably to spawn. Perhaps this charr had decided that the lake was preferable to the fjord, or perhaps it had been caught when Fox River froze. More than a few fish were trapped that way, forced to winter over in the deep waters of the lake. Ivar also suspected that some of the charr were year-round lake residents, for they were smaller and more brightly marked than their silvery seagoing brothers.

He untangled the frozen fish and threw it over beside his pack. He paused for a moment to breathe some warmth back into his hands; then he went back to pulling. Soon another, larger fish appeared, perhaps 8 pounds, heavy and thick.

He pulled out two more 10-pounders before he reached the end of the net. He stacked the four fish to one side, pulled on his gloves and slapped his hands against his shoulders as he walked to the farthest ice hole. After a few minutes of hauling on stiff rope, he had dragged the net beneath the ice again.

When he walked back to the pile of fish, Naika was also there . . . nose on her paws, about 1 millimeter away from a silver fin. She did not look up at his approach, but she did manage one tiny tail-tip wag by way of greeting. Obviously she could have demolished at least one fish while he had been oc-

*Arctic charr, locally known
as "Svalbard salmon"*

cupied, but not so much as a tooth gouge marred the frozen beauty of the nearest charr.

When he spoke to her, the tip of her tail vibrated, but her eyes never left the fish. She watched until the last charr disappeared into his backpack. He shrugged into the pack, heavy and awkward with frozen fish. When he was ready, he looked around for Naika and saw her clear across the lake, playing hockey solitaire with the piece of ice as puck. He left, knowing she would follow.

Naika caught up with him when he stopped to put on his skis. The short light of day was already fading into crimson twilight as he worked his way down the path onto the shelf of land at the shore. He retrieved the two trap frames he had left against the rocks, adding to his awkward burden.

He shuffled along the rough shoreline slowly. Naika ranged ahead, sniffing and watching and listening, senses quivering with messages he lacked the equipment to receive. He moved his shoulders sharply, trying to shift one fish which insisted on digging into his spine. The fish gave grudgingly. He skied on, long slow movements more like walking, his eyes on the trail immediately in front of him.

Naika was casting about a short blind canyon that opened onto the flatland ahead. Her low, penetrating growl snapped Ivar's eyes forward; the hairs on the back of his neck stirred, for that primal canine growl meant bear.

Naika quartered back and forth on a spot near the mouth of the little canyon, nose to the ground, alert and walking with springs in her legs. He dropped the trap frames and unslung the Mauser before he moved forward.

The first sign he saw was his own back trail, ski tracks shadowing the clean snow. But on top of his trail were the wide pad marks of a polar bear. Without wind to fill in the marks, there was no way of judging how old the tracks were.

He knelt and studied the ground where the bear's track overlaid his own. His scent and Naika's must have attracted the bear. It had crossed and recrossed their trail, making a mosaic of pad prints in the snow.

He backtracked the bear for 50 feet. The trail led from the shoreline but did not return. He studied the dark waters of the fjord and saw a large floe a mile or so out. The nomadic ice had brought him the first white bear of the season.

He returned to where the bear's tracks cut his own, then followed the large, long-clawed prints to the mouth of the blind canyon. He stared up into the cluttered chute but saw nothing. He made no move to follow the tracks; they led into an ambusher's paradise.

He turned away from the canyon, back to the rocks where he had left the trap frames. He hesitated, then left the traps against the rocks. Some other day when he was not so burdened he would retrieve them. Right now, he did not want to encounter a polar bear while he had frozen fish and awkward traps hampering him.

As he skied across the flatlands below Fox Valley, he measured the end of the Arctic day with eyes that missed nothing. The twilight was deeper now, the sky a cold cerulean bowl foreshadowing an endless frigid night. And into that night would come the heavy-bodied, light-footed bears. If he were to survive, he must walk even more lightly than the hungry white shadows.

Night

The wind slammed the side of the cabin like a savage hand, jerking Ivar out of two hours of sleep that had been riddled with nagging dreams. He had been bothered by something as he fell asleep, but he had dismissed the sense of unease without pursuing its source. As he sat upright on the bed, encased in his sleeping bag, he remembered the detail that had eluded him—the boat.

Now, in early December, the wind screamed in harsh, continuous cacophony around the corners and past the shuttered windows of Main Cabin, but above the noise he could hear the hollow crunching roll of the fiberglass boat as it rocked back and forth in the raging wind, tethered only by a light chain wrapped around a beach boulder.

In the last few twilight days, the bay in front of the cabin had frozen; the boat would be useless until summertime. In his rush to begin trapping he had forgotten the boat, and as he crawled out of his warm cocoon, he realized that the oversight would cost him some comfort now.

A cold nose pressed against his bare feet as they touched the floor, and Naika's tail thumped a welcome. He patted her automatically, but did not invite her to join him. Without bothering to light a lamp he pulled on trousers, boots and parka. Nor would he take a flashlight outside; he needed both hands for the job ahead.

He pulled open the door that separated the living quarters from the storeroom and was stung by a cloud of snow. Somewhere a nail must have worked loose, or a piece of tar paper had been ripped off by the clawing wind, giving entry to an

Night shot of polar bear just outside cabin

astringent mist of snow crystals. Snow coated every exposed surface in the storeroom already, and the storm had barely begun. It looked as though the first storm of winter would qualify as a real son of a bitch.

He yanked the parka hood up over his head and waded across the room through several inches of powdery snow. He soon discovered the chink. The door was ajar. The gap was fingernail thin, but with a hurricane driving the snow, the room would quickly be filled. He scraped the snow away from the doorframe, slid outside and jerked the door shut behind him.

The Arctic darkness mixed with the driving white snow made a seething, slate-colored stew that obliterated all landmarks. There was neither sky nor ground, only gravity and the pealing wind.

He stood for a moment, adjusting himself to the storm, locating the boat by its sound as it struggled against the chain. The banging noises reassured him that the boat was where he expected it to be, a bit to the left and about 100 feet from the cabin. He studied the storm, measuring its intensity until a sudden gust pushed him against the cabin wall. Cursing the bitter cold darkness and the boat and himself, he opened the storeroom door just enough to get his arm in. He felt along the wall until he found a coil of rope and grabbed it, then shut the door hard. He tied one end of the rope to the cabin before he pushed off into the storm.

When he stepped outside the shelter of the cabin wall, the storm sucked the breath from his lungs and threw him to the ground as though he had neither weight nor strength. He clutched the coiled rope and tried to stand again, but as he scrambled to his knees, he realized that he was playing a losing game of surface areas and wind velocity. As long as he tried to stand the wind would win.

He began to crawl toward the place where the boat banged against rocks.

He had crawled 15 feet when he stumbled across Svarten lying almost completely covered by the snow. The big black husky snarled, then caught the scent of his master and was quiet. Snow had piled up along Svarten's spine, and the dog had no intention of displacing that white insulation for anything less than a polar bear. Not that a bear was likely to be wandering about; in an Arctic hurricane, any sane animal denned up.

Ivar crawled on, groping around obstacles. The wind seemed to suck all the oxygen from the air; he panted like a distance runner. His eyes stung and watered and his eyelashes kept freezing his lids shut. He scrubbed them open a few times, then bowed to the inevitable and let them freeze shut. The storm would be his compass. As long as he kept the wind on his right and headed for the sound of the boat being smashed against rocks, he did not need his eyes.

He had crawled more than 40 feet when the wind jumped a full notch up the scale. He lost the sound of the boat. His first fear was that the strengthened wind had torn it loose from its chain. Then he heard the hull crash, and in his mind he could see the light fiberglass shell dancing in midair before the wind like an awkward balloon at the end of the thin chain. Cursing, he clawed his way down to the shore.

With the crown of his head, he found the rock to which the boat was chained. For a few seconds his curses almost matched the howl of the wind. But he needed his breath for more productive work. He groped with one hand for the boat chain, found it straining, fairly humming with the force of the wind. He tied the free end of his rope to the chain. There was very little slack left in the rope, but it was enough. The wind grabbed the frozen rope and slapped him across the face. He did not bother to curse this time. He grabbed the chain and crawled blindly toward the boat.

The boat crunched to the ground again just as he reached its bow. The loud report so close to his head was a warning; if he were not careful, the next time the boat might come down on him. He backed up a few feet and began grubbing for rocks to weight the boat down. He found a fist-sized rock and worked it free, then used it to hammer larger rocks loose from the frozen ground. Each rock he freed was pitched into the boat, which was now spending only part of its time in the air. He worked until he began to believe that he had always been hammering on rocks while the freezing wind hammered on him.

Finally he had the bow weighted down so that it no longer rolled. He stretched out on the ground to rest. In the relative calm behind his arms he breathed quickly, then more slowly, licking lips salty with sweat or blood—at the moment he was too winded to care which. As his breathing returned to normal, he discovered that it was really rather comfortable there, all things considered. The rocks and snow were not as cold as they had first seemed, and if he kept his head down, he could breathe quite nicely. He would celebrate by taking a little rest. . . .

But his small quiet alarm was triggered after a moment. He was not a husky. He could not sleep under a blanket of snow without freezing to death.

He pushed himself to his knees in the shelter of the boat and resumed grubbing for rocks. One rock as big as a cantaloupe slipped from his grip and blew away in the wind like a ptarmigan feather. But he finished the job and began the long crawl back to the cabin, using the now stiff rope as his guide. He kept the wind on his left cheek, but he must have been slightly off course, for he crawled right over Surly lying buried in the snow. The big dog lived up to his name, snarling his anger at being so abruptly disturbed. Ivar yelled back until Surly settled down and it was safe to crawl by him.

In the lee of the cabin, he stood up slowly, knees aching and bruised. He eased the storeroom door open, then banged it shut and leaned against the cold wood. But as tired as he was, he could not go back to bed yet. In a few hours the wind would die, only to be reborn and blow with renewed fury from the opposite direction. Then the storeroom door would have to take the brunt of the hurricane. If the door were not secure, he would wake up with snowdrifts in his bed.

With clumsy hands he lowered a long, heavy board into place across the door. The fit was tight, as it was meant to be; he had to hammer the board down for the last few inches. Tomorrow he would have to sweep up all the snow and plug any other leaks the hurricane had found or made. But that was tomorrow. Right now he was too tired to do anything more strenuous than fall into bed. In slow motion he peeled off his frozen clothes and crawled into his sleeping bag, ears still ringing with the violence of the storm.

The hurricane died while he slept, but it was followed by another storm, an ordinary Arctic blizzard in which the wind never varied its direction. For three days he was shut up in the cabin, except for one bone-chilling outing to feed the huskies. He killed the crawling hours mending harness, washing clothes and laying them in the storeroom where the wash water froze and could be shattered off, whittling sticks for traps and talking to Naika. Halfway through the blizzard, the wind snapped the antenna he had rigged for his radio, and he lost the one-way company of Radio Luxembourg.

He slept as much as he could, and when he became totally bored, he made a month's supply of bread, kneading the dough furiously to loosen muscles tense with inactivity.

The third morning was much like the first two, with the

wind wailing laments to the dark absence of dawn. He lay for half an hour in his bed, then decided that he had earned another raid on his store of books. He rolled out, lighted the lamp and fire, made a big breakfast and a full pot of coffee and sat down near the fire with the book he had nibbled at on and off through the storm. Scarlett and Rhett were locked in a mad embrace over his cooling oatmeal when he sensed that something had changed. He puzzled for a moment, then realized that the wind no longer shook the cabin.

The chair grated loudly in the silence as he pushed back from the table and went to the door. The blizzard had blown the last twilight out of Hornsund, leaving behind an unbroken expanse of darkness and snow. At the edge of visibility he saw a small heap of snow shift and then explode as Svarten lifted his nose into the dying wind and howled a long, rich, rising note. One by one other heaps of snow moved as the team roused itself.

Ivar returned to the table and closed *Gone with the Wind* with a mixture of reluctance and eagerness. He had read the book a half-dozen times since discovering it that first winter in a box of books at Main Cabin, yet its magic still held him. It was always good for at least one winter storm and sometimes two. Once he had read it from cover to cover, wrapped in his sleeping bag, getting up only to refill the lamp, stoke the fire or fix himself some food. But now, after long days of enforced thumb-twiddling, he was eager to be out and doing. He pulled on his heavy clothes and walked out into the icy aftermath of the storm.

The distinctive sound of an ax chopping into frozen seal brought the huskies yowling to the ends of their chains. They stood on their hind feet and leaned against their thick collars, dancing in anticipation of the coming meal. When he approached, arms full of 2-pound chunks of seal meat, the huskies made enough noise to put a hurricane to shame. He threw the

Svarten

meat deftly, putting each chunk within reach of only one dog. As the meat was snatched out of the air, the noise subsided to steady gnawing punctuated by warning snarls.

The seal vanished like snowflakes in a fire.

When the huskies were finished, Ivar moved among them, ruffling cold fur and talking to those that appreciated human companionship. As always, Svarten leaned against him, ears raised to catch every nuance of tone. For once, even Surly and the stolid Norwegian bachelor brothers, Bumpsa and Grisen, seemed to welcome him for more than the food he had given them. Surly even wagged his tail twice. No wags out of Bumpsa and Grisen, though. They were strong, those two, but interested only in eating, sleeping and working. Lazy, the fifth husky, barely lifted his ears at Ivar's voice.

After eating, though, all the huskies were restive; the unbroken snow beckoned to them. He had allowed the huskies off their leads two at a time, but they had not had a real blood-singing run in front of the sled. They would be full of the devil when the time came to drag out the harness, Svarten in particular. His amber-yellow wolf's eyes watched Ivar's every move, plainly hoping that the harness would miraculously appear.

Ivar returned to the cabin and gathered up his gear—a sackful of ptarmigan heads for trap bait, a shovel to dig the frames out of the snow, the Mauser and a box of shells. And Naika, of course.

Outside the cabin he loaded the rifle. The cartridges made a full brassy ring as he slipped them into the magazine. The bolt moved smoothly, pushing a round into the chamber. At that sound, Svarten strained against his collar. He was a dog who loved the rifle; he knew its use. He danced at the end of his chain, tail high and waving, every movement a plea to be invited along. When Ivar and Naika disappeared around the cabin, Svarten put his nose to the stars and howled. The sound haunted Ivar for as long as he could hear it.

The air was absolutely still as he pushed his skis along an arc toward the Fox Valley flatlands, where he had laid out his first trapline. The fresh snow, packed by the wind, squeaked beneath his weight. Overhead, stars glinted cold and hard against the bottomless sky. For an hour at midday, the stars would be lost in a faint wash of slate light, but for the rest of the day, the stars would be there, pinholes in the shroud of Arctic night.

He skied quickly, using body and poles in a rhythm that was as natural to him as walking. Naika worked to keep up and at the same time explore the nooks and holes along the trail. In the low spots, the snow was several feet deep, packed by the relentless winds. The high areas were almost bare. An intense cold fell from the brittle sky as man and dog moved across the snow, pushing the shapeless night before them.

The first trap was close to the cabin, surrounded by snow. He could see that the frame still hung poised on its prop. He looked back to make sure that Naika had not followed before he skied over to check the trap.

The snow had built up in small mounds around the wooden square, added girth to the outer edge of each rock on the trap but left the area under the trap relatively free of new snow. The bait was untouched. He did not change the bait, although wind and cold had dried the ptarmigan head. The less he handled the bait, the better the results. Even though he took the precaution of keeping a pair of gloves in a box of ptarmigan feathers and using only those gloves when working with trap or bait, foxes were notoriously quick to pick up even the most tenuous foreign scent. The trap was highly visible, close by a well-used fox trail. And fox curiosity was great; it would be a rare fox that overlooked this intrusion into its domain. Once the ptarmigan tidbit was scented, the trap should do its work, especially now, at the beginning of the season.

Early winter was the time of the runners, young foxes on their own for the first time. They were full of energy and curiosity and hunger, ranging far and wide in a pristine world. Those runners would be the first to discover the stone-weighted traps. Later, after the most unwary runners had been caught, trapping would slow down. Only the wily adults and cautious offspring would be left. Then Ivar would have to be much more careful in guarding against the least scent and set the triggers to the lightest touch. Arctic foxes were both quick and bright; they lived by their wits and an innate understanding of the icy land. His traps were only one of the many obstacles they must negotiate in order to survive.

The best of the foxes, those that survived their summer as kits and their first winter as runners, knew that polar bears usually left more than enough to feed a fox, but it was prudent to wait until the bear left the kill. Baby seal in spring were a fox feast, but it was wise to make sure that the mother seal was nowhere near. Later, eggs and chicks made delectable meals, but adult geese could stun or kill with their powerful wings.

The surviving foxes also learned that wooden overhangs weighted with rocks were poor hunting spots, and the scent of man was anathema.

In Ivar's first season, a bold and hungry runner learned the glories of the Main Cabin garbage can. He would steal or beg tidbits from Ivar, but never came within arm's reach. If Ivar was alone, the runner followed him as he scouted trap sites.

The fox was not entirely without survival instincts, though. He was wary of the huskies. He seemed to know when they were tied; he brazenly trotted by them, just outside the circle of snapping and snarling, teasing them. But he disappeared when any of the huskies were loose. He was brassy, but he was not stupid.

Ivar worried over what would happen when he started trapping. Runner was just the sort of fox who would charge in at the first scent of ptarmigan. And he was too much a pet. He never talked to Ivar or let Ivar touch him, but they understood each other. Ivar knew he did not want to find Runner frozen beneath a trap. Yet Ivar could not abandon his trapline because of one foolish fox.

Ivar decided to teach Runner how to survive.

On a spongy section of tundra in front of the cabin, Ivar set up a trap, but left off the stones. Runner, as always, watched with his alert, black-button eyes. Ivar talked as he worked, explaining that the trap was dangerous. It made no impression on Runner. As soon as Ivar fixed the ptarmigan head, Runner was up off his haunches and trotting toward the baited trap. Ivar yelled and yanked and the trap slammed into the tundra. Runner took off, stopped a dozen yards away, then began mincing back toward the heavenly scent of the ptarmigan. If Runner learned at all, it would have to be the hard way.

Ivar rigged the trap again, still without stones. Then he walked off about 30 yards and sat down to wait. Runner approached the trap on tiptoe, then flashed in to take the bait. The wooden trap frame crashed down, flattening him. Ivar ran for the trap, hoping that the foolish little creature was not hurt.

Just as Ivar reached for the frame, Runner wriggled out and staggered off. In a few seconds, he was running fast and strong for the nearest pile of rocks. Ivar raised the baited trap and withdrew to wait.

Eventually, Runner returned. Ivar watched as the fox circled the trap, black nose twitching, every muscle alert. Runner studied the trap from every possible angle—except underneath—

before he trotted away. Ivar left the trap up for a few days, but Runner ignored it. He seemed no worse for the lesson. He was as arrogant as ever, waving that white flag of a tail under the huskies' noses, driving them all to slavering distraction.

Runner followed Ivar the rest of that winter and into spring. Many times Ivar saw his tracks around the traps, but Runner had learned his lesson very well. He was probably still somewhere up in the mountains, siring kits that would not go near a flat frame tipped on edge.

The cold air ached in Ivar's throat as he moved away from the unsprung trap. As he skied toward the next trap, he could hear the sea ice creak and groan as it sagged on the outgoing tide.

He strained his eyes into the moaning darkness, but saw nothing. He was alone inside the womb of his limited senses. The polar night had swallowed up all creatures, digested them in a rumble of ice. It was one of those times when he questioned whether he himself lived or whether he was merely a flickering dream born of icy indigestion.

With a surge of impatience, he shook off the numbing sense of complete isolation; it was too soon to let sunless days get to him. He was definitely alive, and if he wanted to stay that way he had better keep his mind on his business. Experience and instinct told him that the sea ice was heavy enough to support wandering bears.

He checked his surroundings again. To the limit of his night vision, the snow lay in an undisturbed blanket. No movement, no tracks. He listened, breathing quietly through the cold that ached in his throat, heard no sound save the restive sea ice. But ice noise and night could conceal a multitude of living dangers.

He closed his eyes and held himself perfectly still, searching for the least indication that his unnamed senses had discovered what eyes and ears had missed. Nothing. No malaise, no thin, uneasy feeling of being watched by other life.

He opened his eyes and skied to the next trap, all senses alert. He knew he was most vulnerable checking traps alone in the darkness, when Naika's ears and exceptional nose were 100 yards distant. He was on his own, dependent on human senses that were no match for those of the polar bear. In the endless night, he had learned to rely on information that came to him from below the usual sensory level. Maybe it was the presence of other life within the sphere of his own life that warned him, or maybe it was a sound or scent so subtle that he perceived it only unconsciously. Whatever it was that triggered his awareness, he was grateful. It had saved his life many times.

Naika was waiting quietly, patiently, on the trail. She rose to greet him and nuzzled the sack that hung over his back, checking to see if there was something in it she should know about. Satisfied that there was not, she loped ahead, barely indenting the packed snow for all her weight and claws. He followed, the squeaking passage of his skis overlaid by the complaining sea ice.

The first trapline check was a long and fruitless one. The storms had flattened some of the traps; others had drifted so full of snow that he had to dig them out and relocate them on higher ground. Twelve wearying hours of darkness and digging and digging and darkness. By the time he had completed the circular trek, he was clumsy with cold and hunger. The billion stars overhead gave small light and less comfort—it was cold enough to freeze mercury, to say nothing of blood.

He skied forward eagerly, anticipating the rewards of Arctic labor, fire and hot food and coffee laced with Scotch.

He reached the flat coastal ice foot halfway between Fox

Valley and the cabin. The disappointingly empty packsack was crumpled on his back beneath the weight of his rifle. He disliked carrying the Mauser like that, but he could make no speed otherwise. And the quick tempo of his ski poles crunching into snow spoke urgently of his need to be home.

For all his haste, he was alert. His eyes strained into the darkness, scanning rocks and sea ice, seeking bear sign. No movement, no danger yet. He stared around intently. The new snow magnified starlight, giving the land an eerie blue glow.

Naika lagged behind. She had covered twice the distance he had, and she was tired. Her tail had drooped until it was level with her back. Suddenly she stopped, and her low growl curled down Ivar's spine.

Bear.

He stopped immediately, slipped the rifle off his back. He knew that the bear was close, for Naika had caught its scent on the wind. But he had no idea where or how close. As he thumbed the safety off, he spoke softly to the vague dark blur that was Naika. She moved up beside him, staring into the night, head lifted a little to catch another scent. The bear must be out of sight, probably beyond the rocky rise 80 yards away. His eyes could not see the rise, but he had traveled this trail many times.

Naika was silent now, still sniffing the small breeze, and cocking her head from side to side, trying to locate a sound he could not hear. He stabbed his ski poles into the snow and knelt to undo the bindings on his boots. He worked with one hand, keeping the rifle ready in the other and watching the tiny circle of land he could see. No movement. Then he heard, far off, faint, the low sounds of a prowling bear. Naika answered, deep in her chest, uneasy yet excited. She loved the hunt, but she also understood its dangers.

Freed of the skis and poles, he shifted the rifle to his right hand and walked forward, calling very softly to Naika to follow. She trotted stiff-legged, head up.

Ivar circled toward the shoreward side of the rise, looking for tracks. He had to know where the bear was. Some bears avoided or ignored man, but the odds for either were not of an order to encourage carelessness. He had no desire to kill, only to know location, and if there were more than one bear. He paused, slowed his breathing, listened for another sound that would locate the bear.

Nothing.

He advanced another ten steps and stopped again. This time he could hear low snuffling bear sounds. In his mind he could see the bear somewhere on the other side of the rise, aware of life approaching, head swaying on long supple neck, testing the air, waiting.

Naika growled again, but he made no move to silence her. If she could discourage or spook the bear, fine. Unless there was no choice, hunting polar bear in the polar night was plain stupid. Naika growled, loud and rumbling, a sound that released more adrenaline into Ivar's blood. If the bear was going to bolt, it would do so now.

But the bear stood its ground, out of sight, over the rise, wrapped in night. Then he heard the bear huff loudly. The fur along Naika's back rose like a black fan. She flowed to the base of the rise and stopped, a shapeless shadow among all the other shapeless rock shadows.

Ivar swore silently. He had no desire to take on a thousand pounds of aggressive bear when he could not see more than 12 feet ahead. He shifted the rifle to his left hand and pried a stone from the slope at his feet. The stone arced silently over the rise. Naika exploded into eager yaps and charged forward. He called her back, but her excitement drowned whatever small noises a retreating bear might make. He held his breath, hand clamped over Naika's muzzle, listening with every sense of his body and mind.

Finally he heard the bear. He moved up the slope to hear better, but still could not be sure where the bear was. He had to know. The bear was between him and the only route to the cabin. The ice foot that was the trail was narrow, too narrow; it would be impossible either to avoid the bear or wait for it to wander off. The longer he waited, the colder he became. Soon he would not be able to depend on his body, his reflexes. His feet were numb, his bones sharp and cold with hunger.

Yet he waited, listening and hoping and motionless. The few squeaks and crunches he heard were inconclusive—the bear could be backing off or circling around or climbing the ridge. It was time to take the initiative again.

He moved as quietly as he could up the remaining 10 yards to the top of the rise. When he breasted the small hill, the spot where the bear should have been was empty. He glanced right, toward the frozen fjord. Empty. A flicker of movement, no more, to his left.

He spun and faced the white bear less than 15 feet away, lunging from behind a boulder, cat-fast and deadly.

His shot was reflex. He snapped the Mauser forward at arm's length and pulled the trigger. The rifle barrel seemed to touch the point of the bear's shoulder as the muzzle flashed, and the 300-grain lead bullet slammed into bone and through the heart.

The impact of the shot lifted the bear off its right front paw and threw the animal sideways. The bear went down without a sound, rolling over and over down the unbroken snow slope.

Before the bear stopped rolling, Ivar whipped the rifle bolt and jacked in another round. The muzzle flash had blinded him for a few seconds. He held the rifle ready as his eyes began to readjust. Then he saw Naika growling and snarling around the bear that lay bonelessly against a boulder.

As the last echoes of the single shot faded, he listened to the silence. Was there another bear? Was this one dead? No sound or movement but Naika stalking, circling the bear with low growls. Naika was not certain either.

He moved to his left along the crest of the rise, checking again the rocks where the bear had hidden. Even the quick glimpse he had of the lunging bear made him think it was a male, therefore probably alone. But if the bear was a female, with a near-grown cub or even two, the threat was not ended with one death. Moving cautiously, breath quick and shallow, rifle halfway to his shoulder, he listened to the darkness.

He circled 50 feet to the left to examine the bear's tracks. The bear had been alone. The first wanderers of the dark usually were, but usually was not good enough when dealing with polar bears.

He doubled back on the slope to the motionless bear. Naika was still holding her distance, worrying the bear with growls and stiff-legged charges that stopped just short of the thick white fur.

With the threat of a second attack diminished, he decided to risk the loss of his night vision. From the pocket of his parka, he produced a flashlight. Holding it in one hand, but not switching it on, he approached the bear cautiously. He circled the bear at a distance of 10 feet, rifle trained on the long white neck.

Naika's growls increased as he walked up to the bear's head, partially buried by snow that had drifted in the lee of the rock. He switched on the light. The cold had sapped some of the strength from its beam, but the effect was still dazzling against the clean snow and pure white fur of the bear. The light picked up silver tones in the fur, gave it texture and depth. As he swept the beam across the bear, he spotted at once the small crimson entry wound, just forward of the massive shoulder. A fine shot, for reflexes—but then, the range had been point-blank.

The spot of light swept back up to the wedge-shaped head, where ebony eyes shone blankly. He extended the rifle barrel until it touched an unprotected eye. No movement, no flicker.

The bear was indeed dead.

For the first time since he had heard Naika's primal growl, he began to relax. Using his teeth, he pulled off a glove and touched the silvery-white gleaming fur. Beneath his chilled fingers, the long white hairs felt cool. He worked his fingers into the pelt, seeking warmth. And there was warmth, but as he touched it he could sense it dissipating into the polar night.

Ivar stood and swept the beam of light along the bear. Male, rather small, probably no more than 700 pounds. But he had not killed a female, and he was grateful for that. The bear's fur had the fine white glow of health. The winter coat had filled in; there was no yellowing of age on the chest or along the legs. It was a good pelt, well worth the taking. No waste here, no regrets.

He snapped off the light and stepped back, savoring the understanding that his life had been at stake and he had won. Even as he consciously weighed the experience, the rush of adrenaline was fading, diminishing, gone. He moved slowly to a nearby rock and sank down on it. Resting the rifle against his inner thigh, he fumbled in his parka pocket and finally produced a sack of tobacco and a flat package of papers. His fingers were clumsy with cold; it took three attempts to roll a reasonable cigarette. A match flared in the night, then went out, leaving behind a warm red glow at the base of a curl of smoke. He drew deeply, exhaled, drew again, smoking quietly in the dark.

Naika, satisfied that the bear would not move again, trotted over and sat down between Ivar's legs. Her nervous panting made warm clouds in his face as he rubbed her ears and spoke quietly to her. The words had no meaning for her, but their gentle affection made her tail brush rhythmically across the snow. Around them the air began to stir as though awakened by the half moon rising over Missing Mountain. While he finished his cigarette, shadows shifted, dissolved, reformed, adjusting to the silver fall of moonlight. A new land emerged, larger yet still mysterious, edged by darkness.

Ivar flipped the cigarette away and stood wearily. He had a lot to do and no adrenaline to help. The bear must be covered until he could return with the dogs to drag the carcass back to Main Cabin. If the bear were left unprotected, other bears might find and eat the carcass. In the long Arctic night, no source of protein was ignored.

Shouldering the rifle, he moved woodenly up the rise to get his shovel, calculating the hours between work and rest. He had been up since six; if he worked very quickly, he might be home by midnight.

After six hours of sleep, Ivar dragged himself out of the warm down womb and ate a fast breakfast. There had not been enough snow to do a proper job of covering the bear. Worse, a wind had come up as he slept. He had to get back before scavengers ruined the pelt.

When he appeared outside the cabin, harness in hand, the huskies went wild. Svarten did his best to keep order during the harnessing, but he could not be everywhere at once. Bumpsa and Grisen, normally affable, took a sudden and virulent dislike to being harnessed together. Ivar waded in and restored order with a few kicks and a multitude of curses. The huskies separated, unscathed.

The harness was another matter. That thirty-second tantrum had tied an unbelievable number of tight knots in the stiff leather. His invective soared as he tried to pick frozen knots apart with rapidly freezing fingers; he wished he had kicked Bumpsa and Grisen all the way around the cabin—twice.

Ivar knew that the only way to control a team of huskies was to convince the dogs that he was the meanest son of a bitch around. Huskies were not lapdogs. They would kill each other if he did not stop them. At first he had been afraid that he would injure the dogs if he kicked them apart, so he used his hands. Then, one day on the trail, two of his dogs turned on each other. He had screamed at them and screamed at them. Useless. Surly had the other dog's head between his jaws and would not let go. Ivar pounded on Surly's head with his fist, but Surly did not even flinch. Finally Ivar kicked Surly hard enough to lift the big husky out of his tracks. Surly let go and started chewing ice from between his pads as though nothing had happened. The other dog had a long gash right above the eye, but did not seem bothered by it.

Ivar was not as lucky. When he tried to untie the harness knots, he could not. He had broken at least one of the slender bones in the back of his right hand. He turned the team around and headed back to the cabin, tangled harness and all. His hand was very painful, but that was not what worried him. He could not hold, much less aim, his rifle and it was the peak of bear season.

By the time Ivar reached the cabin, his hand had swollen to the size of a melon. He had broken and set his own bones before —usually fingers—but when he tried to straighten the hand bones out, the pain made him dizzy. He did what he could—and waited. For two weeks he was nearly helpless. Until the pain wore off, he would have cheerfully ground up Surly and fed him to the krill.

Yet Ivar would not have traded his troublesome huskies for the best snowmobile on Spitsbergen. He would rather cater to a capricious team of dogs than to a smelly collection of aluminum and cold-rolled steel. But he did get goddamned tired of untying harness knots.

He worried the last knot loose and put Svarten into the lead position. The harness was simple; a single trace connected to the sled, with dogs tied in staggered pairs on either side of the main line.

Svarten was clearly the leader. Surly was clearly the rear guard, where his long teeth and vile disposition encouraged any laggards to hold the pace. Naika was not harnessed. She ran loose behind the sled unless she was needed to help with an unusually heavy load.

Ivar gave a final check to the harness, his ski bindings and the gear strapped to the sled. When he slung his rifle over his back and picked up the towrope that trailed behind the sled, the huskies whined eagerly. He took a firm grip on the knotted end of the rope. His command to run was barely out of his mouth before Svarten leaped forward, nearly yanking the rest of the huskies off their feet.

In seconds, the dogs were towing him and the nearly empty sled in a mad rush over the dark and frozen land.

For the first mile he did nothing more than hang on, knowing that there was nothing else he could do. The huskies were wild with their first run of the season. They would respond to nothing but their own pounding blood. The snow covered most rocks, but he still had to strain into the darkness, ready to swing out on the towrope to avoid boulders and bare spots. If he should get dumped now, the dogs would not stop for him. He hung on, knees flexed, cheeks burning, silent laughter curving his cold lips. Neither cold nor darkness nor hidden rocks could mar the sheer, rushing beauty of the huskies and the hissing skis.

At the end of the first mile, the team's all-out run settled into a steady, hard-pulling gallop. It was time to see if Svarten remembered his master's voice. Ivar yelled for Svarten to veer right. The big black dog responded promptly. Ivar called for a left turn. Svarten moved quickly to the left. Ivar was pleased, but he knew better than to press his luck by asking the team to stop. It would take a bit more running before the huskies would listen to such a ridiculous request. Better to give them their heads now, so they would not be fractious when he loaded the bear on the sled.

The second mile passed somewhat less quickly, though sled runners and skis still hissed with speed. Svarten was loping now, a long fluid movement that kept the traces taut. His head was held high, ears forward; he was born to run and he knew it. The team worked largely without sound, except when Lazy lagged slightly. Then Surly snarled and nipped and Lazy yipped back into place.

As they approached the rise, he waited for the dogs to show that they scented bear. When the team continued its ground-eating lope, he felt the beginnings of relief; the bear probably had not been disturbed. Just to be sure that there were no live bears downwind of the carcass, he let the dogs run before the wind for another half mile before he called out for Svarten to go left. Svarten immediately bore left, beginning a long arc across the flat coastal shelf as Ivar yelled encouragement from the end of the towrope.

Just as the dogs had half completed the turn and were facing out toward the fjord, a flicker of white flashed from behind a grounded iceberg close to shore. They had surprised a white fox on its scavenging rounds. Ivar saw the fox an instant before the huskies did and screamed for the team to stop, simultaneously kicking sideways and dragging against the towrope to emphasize his command. But Svarten had also seen the fox.

The chase was joined.

Unfortunately, the fox was old and cunning; it knew that its chances of skirting around the team to the safety of shore were zero. The fox veered right, toward the fjord, running belly down away from the shore.

Ivar yelled repeatedly for the team to stop, but Svarten ignored the commands; the fresh smell of fox was irresistible. The big husky leaned right, pulling the team after the fox. Ivar was helpless to do anything more than hang onto the rope and scream curses at the headstrong leader. If Ivar turned loose of the towrope, the dogs might run unchecked for 10 or 15 miles. Svarten flattened out, working hard against the traces, running with great open strides that the other dogs strained to match. But the fox had the advantage. It became a white blur at the edge of vision, fading in and out of the darkness like a dream. The huskies ran on, still picking up speed, giving Ivar bare seconds to discover and avoid rocks leaping out of the darkness. He tried to keep loose, knees flexed, body ready to twist and weave as necessary.

Suddenly Svarten and the rest of the team dropped, the sled thumped loudly and Ivar was airborne over the 30-inch ridge that marked the last of the land and the first of the sea ice. He had known that the ridge would be there—the tide was ebbing—but there was no time to lean back and raise the tips of his skis. A combination of luck and reflexes kept him from cartwheeling over the bay ice. He landed hard enough to make his teeth ache, but he landed right side up.

The bay ice was thick, but it was far from safe. In every direction he could see vague shapes, the remains of summer icebergs frozen into the new ice. Knee-high, waist-high, head-high, they made an obstacle course that he had to negotiate at top speed in darkness. Without real hope of effect, he yelled at Svarten to stop.

He was still yelling when the fox faded through a narrow gap between two low icebergs. Svarten hit the opening flat out. Bumpsa and Grisen were forced up and over the bergs. Ivar hoped the sled would jam between the blocks of ice, forcing the dogs to stop, but Bumpsa's frantic scrambling had tipped the sled onto one runner; it was unceremoniously yanked through by the charging huskies. Ivar was jerked out of position, heading straight for an iceberg. He crouched and swung way out to the right, holding the towrope up to clear the top of the berg. He felt the outside edge of his left ski scrape and heard the thin song of wood against immobile ice. Close.

He breathed deeply and yelled until his throat was cold and hoarse, but he might as well have been shouting encouragement. The fox had faded into view again, a white cloud flying low in front of the silent, racing huskies. He opened his mouth to yell again, then heard something that froze the breath in his throat.

The sound seemed to come from far away, as though someone were slowly pulling nails from green lumber—new sea ice flexing as it gave beneath the combined weight of dogs and sled and man. The fox had led them onto thin ice disguised beneath a layer of snow.

Quickly Ivar swung out to the left, toward heavier ice and the safety of land, pulling and yelling at the team. But the huskies were too strong, the quarry too close. The team plunged on.

Ivar was helpless. If he let go, he would be stranded on the sagging ice. Worse, he would doom the huskies. As long as he hung on, there was a chance that Svarten would respond. The huskies had run at top speed for more than 2 miles; they had to be winded. If only the fox would help out by doubling back toward shore. But what was acute danger for the heavy dogs was utter safety for the little Arctic fox, and the fox knew it.

The ice gave beneath Ivar's skis, stretching like an elastic sheet, humping up in subtle rises that became hillocks. He skied the flexing ice and abandoned the idea of stopping the dogs. Their only hope now was movement, never resting long enough for the ice to give way. And turn the team—he must turn the team.

His urgent command rang out over the ice, was swallowed up in darkness and groaning. He called again and yet again, called until either fatigue or training or the uneasy ice brought Svarten out of his single-minded pursuit of the white fox.

Svarten edged left, slowed, ice rippled and heaved. Svarten plunged forward, tightening the traces as he picked up speed again. Under the hoarse lash of Ivar's voice, the big husky kept the tired team running over the rubbery ice, running in a sweeping arc that pulled them toward shore. By degrees the ice stopped swaying and groaning, and finally Ivar was again dodging icebergs in the bay. When he saw the shore break, he called for Svarten to stop. Svarten did so immediately, a model of fatigued obedience. Cursing the dogs steadily, Ivar forced his cramped fingers to let go of the towrope.

Svarten's head drooped; he did not understand the words, but the tone was scathing.

Ivar stood, flexing his hands to restore circulation, spewing imprecations until his breathing and adrenaline level returned to normal. He looked back over the bay ice, but it was far too dark to spot the cause of all the trouble. He had a mental picture of the sly white fox sitting on its haunches, pink tongue quivering with silent laughter.

And as for you, you little bastard, if I trap you, I'll feed you to the dogs—pelt and all!

With a last dispirited curse, he pulled his mind back to the business at hand. There was still a bear to be dug out and levered aboard the sled and dragged back to the cabin. Then the entire trapline must be checked. Muttering softly, he helped the dogs pull the sled up over the ice lip onto shore. It was going to be a long day.

Ivar skied slowly along the shoreline east of Main Cabin. Behind him was a straight eleven hours of trapline work. Checking downed traps, knocking 80 pounds of rock off wooden boards, resetting triggers, piling 80 pounds of rock back onto tilted frames, watching piles slide off when the last rock was put into place, starting all over again. All but one of the traps was storm-downed; Ivar's packsack contained one lone fox.

Tomorrow he would shut down this trapline and reopen the wide, ragged circle of traps that started behind Main Cabin, curved along the lower edge of Fox Valley and out across the flatlands, then arced down and blended into the coastal trapline just below Fox River. Each day for seven days he would make the same twelve-hour circle. Then he would shut down that trapline and go back on the coast for another week.

He had between eighty and one hundred traps laid out and usually kept half of them open. Yet for all the movement from mountain to flatland to shoreline, he felt as though he were setting the same trap over and over and over again. In the dark, there was so little difference. The icy rocks and square frames and pale snow never varied. Only his body changed, more cold and tired with each dark stone, each dark trap, each dark hour.

But even more than fatigue, the long weeks of night dragged at him as he shuffled away from the last coastal trap. The stars gave some light, as did the cresecent moon sliding down into the frozen sea, but the light was far too thin to feed eyes hungry for the colors of summer. The monotone wind matched the monochrome land, unvarying, uncaring, stultifying. Then an invisible bank of clouds condensed in the west, blotting out the moon and the polar stars. Landmarks and shapes and gradations of darkness all drowned in a tidal surge of featureless night.

His unease opened like a black flower, each petal a separate fear. He stopped suddenly, eyes straining to orient his body. There, that bulge of snow. Was it a rock close by or a hill further off? Was it a ptarmigan or a fox or a bear? Without perspective, there was no way to be sure. But did it matter? Did anything matter in this unreality?

Deliberately, he knelt and checked his ski bindings. The wind blew over his half-turned face, cut coldly across his eyes. The movement and pain reassured him; he was not dreaming, not caught in a shapeless nightmare from which there was no waking.

He stood and turned to face the wind. The rifle slung over his shoulder bumped his side. Another reality. He kicked the stock with his elbow, and the rifle moved again. With his left hand he reached up and touched the strap of the packsack over his other shoulder. The frozen fox, retrieved from a trap hours ago, rested lightly on his hip. He took a shallow breath, and the sound of air being drawn through nostrils crusted with ice calmed him. Still alive, still breathing.

Above the keening wind came the far-off explosion of two ice plates moving together on the force of the tide. The tidal flow was proof that the moon still existed and worked its ways upon the water. Again the far-off grinding crunch.

I exist, and the rest of the world exists. Nothing has changed but the light.

He had known the feeling of nonbeing before, many times, but each time its depth and cutting edge surprised him. During his first winter, it had struck him shortly after the sun set for the last time. He had been alone at Cabin Bay, working a one-man trapline while Fredrik stayed at Main Cabin with the dogs and the Fox Valley trapline.

The night malaise had struck deep and hard. Only his pride had kept him at Cabin Bay for endless days, skiing the traps and grappling with the fact of being totally alone. One night, in the dark cabin, he had cried with the realization that he was afraid and alone and there was little he could do about either. It had been a long, long time since he had last cried; the uncontrolled release of tension and anguish helped. He felt real again, if somewhat chagrined. The Arctic night had scoured him down to raw flesh, but he had found that flesh still existed.

Fredrik and Ivar could have lived together, but neither man had come to the Arctic for companionship. It was just as well; the area around one cabin could not support two trappers. And a small cabin got very much smaller during the dark. It was impossible not to irritate each other. Because Fredrik had encouraged Ivar to come to Hornsund, Fredrik felt responsible for keeping Ivar alive. Every time Ivar did something Fredrik would not have done, there was a loud argument followed by a long silence.

It would have been easier if they did not care about each other. But they did. If possible, Ivar would make the run to Cabin Bay for Christmas. Other than that, they would live alone, each free to meet the Arctic in his own way. They did not even have the comfort of knowing that if one of them was injured, the other would be able to help. Cabin Bay was a long day's trip from Main Cabin. If Ivar could travel that far, he did not need help. As for the loneliness . . . it was simply part of the Arctic night, part of everyone's night.

Ivar stood for a while longer, letting the wind tug at his beard, measuring the loneliness that was the other face of freedom. Then he turned his back to the wind and pushed on for Main Cabin.

The cabin had not changed in his absence, except to grow as cold as the surrounding land. The slanting snow tunnel was still intact. The entry room was still a hallway lined with firewood; the gun rack still held his .22, shotgun and the spare rifle. He put the heavy Mauser into the rack and went through the opposite door, down a narrow corridor to the living-room door.

The room was larger than Bird Mountain's tiny space, but not too large to be heated by the big cookstove along one wall. The rest of the walls were lined with shelves of books, cabinets of food, bed, table, chairs and washbasin. There were three other rooms, cold rooms, down the corridor, but he did not have to see them to know what was there. He had seen it all before, too many times.

He dropped the frozen fox in the corridor, hung his frozen parka on a peg and lit the kerosene lamp. His motions were automatic, part of a routine that was as unvarying as the darkness outside.

He glanced around the room without seeing, then looked again more carefully. What he saw told him that he had become sloppy. Books scattered about, cooking utensils in disarray, salt and sugar and oatmeal and flour containers on the table instead of the cooking shelf, odds and ends in strange places.

And only a blind man could call the breakfast dishes clean.

With a sound of disgust, he began cleaning house. By nature he was orderly; even if he had not been, the Arctic would have changed him. There were too many times when his well-being or even his life depended on being able to find the right thing in the right place. An untidy cabin was a danger signal. The monotonous darkness was nibbling away at his life.

He could understand those first poor Englishmen, the prisoners condemned to death. A seventeenth-century bureaucrat, sensing the possibilities of Spitsbergen, offered the prisoners their lives—if they colonized the island. A boatload of volunteers arrived in late summer. As winter closed in, the choice between death and endless darkness seemed less and less sure. Finally the entire colony lost its nerve. Every last man chose to return to England and the hangman's rope rather than face the soulless night.

He could understand their flight, but he could not agree with it. He knew that fear and the dark were corrosive, and that his own mind could be his worst enemy. But he was here and here he would stay until sunrise. He would endure because he had chosen to do so.

And because there was no other choice.

After three hours of whirlwind work, the elements of his life were restored to their proper places. He did not stop with housecleaning. Though his exterior was polished and orderly, his interior rumbled with hunger. A special dinner was in order, a celebration of . . . well, just a celebration.

Soon the cabin was redolent of roast duck and mashed potatoes and rich brown gravy, hot peaches laced with honey and cinnamon, coffee strong enough to wake the dead. The sound of his chair sliding close to the feast brought Naika out of hiding. The silent, pleading pressure of her eyes breached the residue of darkness in him. He realized that it had been days since he had even spoken to her. Such withdrawal was not only dangerous, it was manifestly unfair. He spoke quietly, apologizing, and he fed her thick scraps of duck. Naika sat

Naika

attentively, tail whisking arcs on the floor, responding as much to his voice as to the succulent food.

When the feast was finished, Naika followed him around while he cleaned up the dishes. She was not underfoot, but neither was she more than inches away. As he draped the dishrag over a nail, she butted him expertly behind the knees. When he turned to face her, she was standing expectantly, ears up and dark eyes alive with play. His hands flashed out and Naika's claws scrabbled across the wooden floor as she evaded him. Soon he and the big dog were rolling and scuffling, Naika determined to pin him to the floor and lick him to death, Ivar wriggling desperately to avoid such an undignified end.

When they were both out of breath, he scrambled to his feet, ending the game. While Naika licked her ruffled fur into place, he made himself a nightcap—tawny Scotch whiskey, smoky and rich, chilled by a piece of glacier ice, ice a thousand years old and dense with the weight of time and tons of compacted snow. The inexorable glacial process had trapped tiny pockets of air within the ice, and as the chunk melted in the Scotch, the air sprang forth with tiny pings and whistles, icy music of the ages playing a bright counterpoint to the crackling fire. For the moment, his world was complete inside the cabin, with fire and light and food and Naika's companionship. Yet he also knew that only a few feet away, night was thick with wind and cold and haunted by emptiness.

As Ivar sipped the last of his Scotch, the silence outside dissolved into a low sound rising and falling in a minor key. The rounded ululations paused, then flowed up the scale again. Svarten's howl was joined by another and another, each different, until five voices blended in eerie harmonics older than man.

Naika stirred, and from her throat poured an answering

song. Ivar put his glass aside and pulled on a jacket. With Naika close behind, he let himself into the snow tunnel that was the cabin's winter exit. When he pushed aside the trapdoor he had set into the snow, a soft drift of crystals powdered his beard and shoulders. The first thing he noticed was the absence of clouds. Countless stars burned across the black bowl of night, outlining the jagged mountains north of Main Cabin.

As he turned toward the south, he saw shimmering green condense out of the darkness, dimming the stars. As though blown by distant winds, the curtain of green light billowed and twisted while the huskies sang their ancient haunting song. A curl of pale blue appeared in the aurora, became a silent fall of sapphire among emerald eddies. Thin topaz streamers ghosted through the cascading light. Then the aurora faded, with only Svarten's rippling elegy to mark its passing. A radiant disk of moon rose, flooding the land with delicate silver light and ebony shadows. For one piercing moment he was at peace . . . then the moment faded and he was shivering and alone and besieged by the terrible beauty of the Arctic night.

He went back inside the cabin and moved restlessly around the living room. After a few minutes, he poured another Scotch and sat in front of the fire, staring at the flames with unseeing eyes.

Ivar worked the traplines through the long December days, measuring time by the growing number of diagonal marks across the face of a curling paper calendar. Except for those marks, and occasional three-fox days on the traplines, there was nothing to tell one week from the next. The inevitable storms swept through the night, churning sky and sea and land into a primal sameness. Clouds lowered and the temperature rose and fat flakes of snow sifted out of darkness. Clouds rose and flew away on a screaming wind that transformed softness into a billion hard crystals scouring ice and rock and mountains alike.

Inside the snow tunnel, he listened to the blizzard hissing overhead, wondering if the storm would ever stop. Christmas was only two days away. He wanted to go to Cabin Bay to visit Fredrik for the holiday. In bad weather, the trip could take several days—if he did not get lost. If he got lost, he would stay lost until the storm ended.

In a storm like this, he should not go at all.

He went back into the cabin and worked over one of the foxes he had brought in from the trapline five days ago. Skinning and preparing a fox pelt was finicky work; the skin was so fragile that he could poke his finger through it. Each unnecessary cut lowered the value of the pelt, yet every last particle of fat and flesh must be scraped off by his finely honed skinning knife. The work required patience, concentration and a very light touch.

Tonight, he lacked the first two requirements. The knife slipped off a bone and drew a thin red line across his knuckle. Cursing his carelessness he washed and disinfected the cut thoroughly, then returned to working on the pelt and worrying about the storm. By the time the skin was stretched inside out over a drying frame, he was no closer to deciding what to do about Christmas than he had been two days ago.

He went to the storeroom for another fox to skin, but returned instead with a prepared pelt, the only blue fox he had taken this winter. He sat by the fire, running his fingers through the fine silken fur, dreaming of another world.

There is a huge ballroom glittering with crystal light and elegant women. A waltz is playing. Graceful couples turn and dip and long dresses flare in smooth curves. When the violins stop, another couple is announced. The woman moves forward, and she is more beautiful than the music and light. Around her shoulders is a blue haze of finest fox. When the music begins again, she floats out onto the floor, smiling up at her partner.

The fire crackled loudly, fracturing his dream. He stroked the pelt once more, then walked back to the storeroom and hung the soft fur carefully. He returned to the living room with dragging feet, wondering what he could do to kill time, short of skinning yet another fox. Finally he pulled his chair over to the radio and began fiddling with the tuner. Usually the aurora interfered with reception, but the aurora seemed to have taken the night off. He found a static-free station which gently sang Norwegian hymns and carols. The effect was not as devastating as he had expected it would be; instead of increasing his loneliness, the music mellowed him.

After a while he settled back on his bunk, radio still playing, and began to read *The Forsyte Saga* for the third time. The bottle of Scotch was close at hand; he drank and smoked and read for several hours, immersed in a glow that short-circuited loneliness. In time he slept, and dreamed.

When he awoke, he remembered the dream . . . Christmas Eve in Norway, a cascade of lights winding down hills to churches radiant with song, winking bulbs glowing on fragrant pine boughs, the rainbow lights of Oslo.

The memory made him ache.

With an effort, he pulled his mind back to the present. He listened for a long moment before he realized that he could barely hear the wind. He smiled; it was too early to leave, but he would not spend Christmas alone.

He lay in the darkness, thinking about the trip to Cabin Bay. West from Main Cabin, across the flatlands to the mouth of Fox River and beyond, to where the fjord opened out onto the frozen sea. The trail bent north from there, zigzagging along the coast, north to the bay just below Torell Glacier's huge ice cliffs. There Fredrik was spending the year, trapping fox and hunting bear, watching storms sweep over the white ocean, reading and sleeping and dreaming his own, unknown dreams.

Ivar slept again and awoke again. The luminous hands on his watch told him it was very early morning on the day of Christmas Eve, but he got up and dressed anyway. He cooked a large breakfast to hold him on the trail, gathered the equipment he would need and loaded the sled. The dogs were up and restless, sensing a run.

When all the equipment was strapped on and the huskies were harnessed, he returned to the cabin. He had let the morning's fire die away while he worked outside, and the living area of the cabin had already been reclaimed by cold. The water in the small sink pail was covered over with a thin sheet of ice, and the walls farthest from the stove had begun to shine with a thin layer of hoarfrost, condensation from the ocean air and the moisture of his own breath.

He scooped the cold ashes from the stove and transferred them to an ash can. The fine gray particles drifted up, tickling his nose. After making certain that the stove was cold, he built coal and kindling and blubber into a neat pile that would be his next fire. The trick was to lay the base in such a way that a single match could start the fire. Almost every time he returned to a cabin, quick heat was merely a convenience. But he did not build so carefully for convenience; he built for the time that a single match could be the division between death and life.

Ritual completed, he gave the cabin one more quick check —windows closed and shuttered securely to keep the driving snow out, utensils and equipment in order, floor swept and refuse removed.

He picked up the Mauser from the rack and automatically checked the load. Ready, waiting. He set the safety and slung the rifle across his back, picked up the harness and quickly checked it for knots or signs of wear.

The sight of the leather straps dangling from his hands brought all the dogs to their feet again. They were as ready as his rifle. Even Surly submitted to the harness with relish. Ivar secured the towrope to a post, preventing the eager huskies from racing off without him while he made one last check of the storeroom. He tested the heavy outer door by slamming his fists against it several times. The door barely quivered. The cabin was buttoned up against all but the most determined polar bear, and short of heavy-gauge steel, there was no way to avoid that type of invasion.

He stepped into his skis and untied the towrope. The team sprang forward before he could say a word. He hung onto the rope and yelled encouragement to Svarten, a dark shadow running silently ahead of four similar shadows. Though he could not see the clouds, he knew that they were overhead, shutting out the stars.

The first burst of speed wore off, and the huskies settled down to a steady, ground-covering trot. When they were well beyond his last fox trap and his hands ached from hanging onto the towrope, he called for Svarten to stop. While the team rested, he flexed his hands, trying to warm unfeeling fingers. Naika came up to him and panted helpfully over his gloves. He took them off and knelt beside her, talking softly and rubbing his fingers underneath her thick fur. She leaned into his touch, rumbling deep in her throat and chewing affectionately on his arm.

After a few minutes he stood and stared out toward the darkness that was the mouth of the fjord, checking unconsciously for signs of weather. He could have seen nearly as much with his eyes closed, but habit was strong.

At first he thought his eyes were teasing him. Off in the distance, almost beyond the limits of even sunlight vision, a string of tiny lights danced and twinkled in the clear air beneath the cloud cover. He closed his eyes, counted softly, then opened them again. The dancing lights remained, just above the ice horizon. Far, far off he heard faint sounds like bells.

For an instant, he thought of Santa Claus—that old fat man heading out from the North Pole, loaded down with goodies. He laughed at the thought, knowing that the lights belonged to seal boats moving along unseen leads through the sea ice beyond Hornsund. Faint bell sounds, then a gust of wind brought more distinct peals. But even after he had identified the crystal sounds, he stood in the icy darkness watching the tiny lights, taking comfort from the proximity of other human beings. He waited for the bells to ring again, but clouds lowered and the hidden ocean stirred. Sea ice shifted, tuning up for its twice-daily winter serenade. Pings and shrieks and hollow booms . . . and eerie, tubalike groans.

Abruptly, he became aware of stinging in his fingertips, the forerunner of frostbite. He pulled on his gloves, picked up the towrope, and called out to Svarten. The dogs surged forward, towing him through the darkness. Soon he fell into the rhythms of night travel, mind half dreaming, body automatically responding to the trail's demands, eyes unfocused because there was nothing to focus on.

The sound of Fredrik's huskies howling a greeting finally brought Ivar fully awake. The door of the cabin opened, making a warm golden rectangle in the darkness. Fredrik greeted him with a wide smile and a few thumps on the back, asking about the trip as he helped tie and feed the dogs.

Christmas; Fredrik and Naika

As Ivar entered the cabin, his mouth watered at the rich food scents. The kitchen area held loaves of fresh bread, buttery crusts reflecting the lamplight, and two fruit pies cooling on the counter. Soup simmered at the back of the stove and a goose thawed in a counter-top pan.

Ivar smiled and set down his pack. A few seconds of rummaging produced a bottle of Black Label Scotch and another of Martell cognac, part of his contribution to the Christmas feast. After they had eaten soup and slices of crusty bread, they sat at the table, sipping Scotch and talking quietly. As the hours passed, Fredrik's tales grew taller and Ivar's sides ached from laughter. There was a snack of spicy sausages and cheese and thick pieces of bread, then more Scotch as they sang their favorite carols. But gradually the sounds faded into a sputtering fire and large yawns.

There was a strangeness about awakening with another human being in the room, and both men were aware of it. They sipped the hot coffee in silence. Later they would talk again, but for now it was enough just to let the coffee slowly penetrate heads thick with last night's drinks.

After a few cups of coffee, Fredrik rose and worked in the kitchen, preparing the goose for the oven. When he was done, he returned to the table with a pot of fresh coffee, some sweet rolls filled with jam, and a chessboard. Morning became afternoon as the two men sat head to head, enjoying the luxury of another human intelligence after months of solitaire and wind. Neither one payed too much attention to the margin of victory or defeat; the companionship was more important than the score.

When the smell of roast goose could no longer be ignored, they broke out another bottle of Scotch, toasting each other's health and fortune. Then they ate soup and apples, goose and gravy, potatoes and carrots, bread and jam and thick fruit pies until their stomachs groaned. They worked off their fullness by cleaning up, knowing that chess or conversation could not thrive in the middle of a messy table. They sat with coffee and cognac; the only sounds were the click of chessmen and an occasional anguished cry when Ivar's aggressive moves brought him afoul of Fredrik's carefully laid traps. When the game was over, they talked quietly from time to time, but neither felt a need to disturb the pleasant silences which gradually claimed them.

They both knew that tomorrow Ivar would leave. They had given each other a fine Christmas; staying for another day or week could not make the gift any brighter.

They were as close as father and son, yet they made few demands on each other. For them, affection or love did not depend on being able to drop in and say hello every day. They used to laugh, softly, over the stories about two trappers living together through the long Arctic night—if only one returned, no one asked too many questions.

Basically, Fredrik and Ivar were loners, and they respected that in each other. The balance of each man's life was delicately struck. One could not depend too greatly on the other, for if disaster came, each would be alone. Each must face Arctic realities with his own unique blend of weakness and strength. This, like so many of the bonds between them, needed no words.

Ivar woke to tantalizing breakfast smells. He washed up hurriedly and packed the sled while Fredrik cooked. As they sat down to eat, Fredrik mentioned that the weather did not feel promising. Ivar listened to the wind, shrugged and cleaned his plate.

Cabin Bay

Fredrik said nothing more. After years of worrying over Ivar, Fredrik had finally decided that the wild hunter opposite him would very likely die young. If Ivar lived until the melt, Fredrik would know when the ship came back to pick them up. If Ivar were not there when the ship came, there was absolutely nothing Fredrik could do about it. So he tried not to worry. Sometimes he even succeeded.

When the dogs were harnessed and ready, Fredrik clapped Ivar's shoulder, wished him a good trip, and curbed a desire to point out that the wind definitely smelled of storm. Ivar knew what Fredrik was thinking and appreciated his restraint. The visit had been too good to spoil by another argument about "unnecessary risks." He gave Fredrik a quick, one-armed hug, then picked up the towrope and called out to Svarten.

As the team pulled him down the small peninsula, he glanced back once, but the cabin had melted back into the land, an indistinguishable darkness in the greater black of night. The wind picked up, blowing steadily at his back, pushing him down the trail between unseen mountains and frozen sea. He leaned against the towrope, letting the dogs do the work and trusting them to warn him of bear or any other dangers of the night. He glanced up at the stars, but found no reference. The sky was opaque with darkness and clouds. The wind was steady and hard, but not yet strong enough to lift the packed snow. He settled back into the monotony of being towed through the seamless dark.

For hours he traveled without thought or real awareness. Then he realized that he was half asleep and the other half ached with cold. He shook off his lethargy and began to ski with the team, lightening their load and getting his own blood moving again. The effect was immediate; he recognized the contours of the trail. Although he could not see the rocky depression in the mountainside that he called Halfway Bowl, he knew it was close by, veiled in darkness. More important, the wind had shifted. He was heading almost straight east, yet the wind was still sending icy fingers down his back.

He turned his head, realizing as he did that he would see nothing but darkness. But his weather sense told him the storm was coming. The wind felt warmer, too warm. With a rising temperature, any change would be for the worse. He gave the dogs a short rest while a bud of worry grew in the back of his mind. He was at least four hours from Main Cabin, but distance was far less important than conditions. If the weather fell apart even a mere half mile from home, he could be a long time getting next to the fire.

He called to Svarten to pick up the pace. Immediately the long-legged husky stretched out. Ivar shuffled along as quickly as he could, trying to lighten the team's load, skiing and sliding across the hard snow. Gradually the clouds dropped down, hiding the team in an icy fog.

The storm caught up with them a mile west of the Fox Valley flatlands. The wind had been peeling off tendrils of packed snow for several hours. The drifting crystals had not slowed him or the team, but new snow would. When the first soft, wet flakes sailed past his head, parallel to the ground and flying before a wind that gusted heavily, he knew that it would be a long way to Main Cabin.

The snow thickened quickly, a heavy wet curtain descending over the land, rippling before the wind in formless waves. The relative warmth of the rising temperature was quickly offset by a dampness unusual in the high Arctic, a dampness which chilled and clung.

Ivar felt the heavy flakes coat his face, thawing on his lips and freezing on his cheeks and eyelids. He prayed that it would get no warmer. He had seen freak winter rainstorms descend on Hornsund. The price of a few hours of warmth was a rigid layer of ice. Until snow covered the glaring landscape, movement was both difficult and dangerous. Animals caught in the rain had an excellent chance of freezing to death when the inevitable subzero cold returned, transforming waterlogged fur or feathers or clothes into crackling jackets of ice.

The wind quickened, strengthened; breathing became difficult. Deep breaths brought in snow; shallow breaths could not compete with the wind, which seemed to suck the air out of his lungs. He pushed ahead anyway, dreading to feel the first raindrops on his face.

The wet snow clung to the ground in spite of the wind's power. Friction dragged at the sled's runners, slowing the team. The dogs had to fight through the mushy new snow for purchase on the frozen trail beneath. He called encouragement, but did not ask for more speed. There was no point in exhausting the dogs this far from the cabin. The huskies were using their lean muscles to the fullest; the rest was up to the weather. Svalbard storms were unpredictable. Some were merely snow squalls that came and went in an hour. Others were windstorms that hung on for days. Both types of storm were uncomfortable and could be dangerous for a man in the open. But storms could be endured. They had to be.

He pumped his legs in rhythmic sequence, skiing beside the sled, slogging through the wet new snow. Even without his weight on the towrope, the team was slowing down. He kept the rope looped loosely about his right wrist, a safeguard against becoming separated from dogs he could barely see through the darkness and racing snow. Every few steps he reached up with one hand and tried to brush the ice from his eyelashes. His reward was fifteen seconds of clear vision and rapidly abraded eyelids. But all he could see was the gray storm swirling around the dark bulk of the sled. If the wind got any worse, he would be lucky to see his feet. He knew that the huskies were ahead only because the sled still moved forward. Slowly. He shouted out praise and encouragement, knowing that the team was working hard. He considered putting Naika and himself into the traces, but abandoned the idea. He would lose more time fiddling with the harness than would be gained by having extra bodies to pull the sled.

Man and dogs slogged on, each wrapped in choking snow and darkness. Ivar no longer told Svarten which way to turn, for in zero visibility the husky's sense of direction was more reliable than a man's. Besides, the wind swallowed any sound a mere man could make. The team moved at a labored trot, strung out invisibly on the leather traces. Ivar became a follower, his entire world a circle with a 3-foot radius. He fought the impulse to scream back at the wind. The choking curtains of snow and wind and darkness were uncomfortable and, to one small part of him, unnerving. But the discomfort must be endured, the claustrophobia suppressed; if he gave way to irrational fear he would be committing suicide. Stop thinking. He plodded on, head down, eyelids frozen shut because it no longer made a difference. One step, then another.

He knew he had reached Fox River when he felt his skis pitch forward over the steep incline of the riverbank. He threw himself backward as he fell. He slid on his back for a few seconds before coming to rest in a snarl of huskies, harness, sled and skis. The snow was soft and deep in the lee of the bank, and it took a few minutes to fight his way upright again.

The huskies, too, were scrambling back to their feet, falling over one another and further tangling harness. Ivar kicked off his skis and jammed the ends into the snow. He stopped to scrub the ice off his eyelids after he banged his shin on the sled. The bank cut off enough wind that he could see perhaps

10 feet ahead. He counted quickly—six dogs. Good. None of them had been run over by the sled. He set about untangling the harness.

The loops and crossed lines were not as bad as he had expected. The dogs were too tired to quarrel; they stood quietly while he sorted them out. The snow still fell and blew heavily, but the rocky banks of the riverbed broke the force of the gale. This was as good a place as any to rest and think.

Once he had untangled the harness behind Svarten, he pushed the big husky down on the snow, gentling him with a few words and a pat on the shoulder. Seeing their leader lying down, the rest of the team promptly curled up, tails over noses to block the insidious snow and provide a small quiet breathing space.

He made his way back to the sled and sank down beside it. Nature had not provided him with a bushy tail, so he had to make do by pulling his parka hood forward. He sat motionlessly, taking stock. In the last two hours, he and the team had barely covered a mile, and even that slow pace had taken its toll. He was tired. Although movement had kept him warm, he knew that sooner or later the cold would suck the last warmth and strength out of him. Above him the storm scoured the flats with casual ferocity. Even in the sheltering riverbed, the world was a dizzying swirl of snow and darkness.

As he sat and enjoyed the luxury of not having to breathe through a screen of snow, he tried to gauge where on Fox River he was. He had kept the wind on his back since the snow began, so he should be about a quarter mile from the seashore, where the river was broad and the banks shallow. But his tumble down the bank told him he must be farther inland. The wind must have shifted a few degrees from west toward south, blowing him up into the entrance of Fox Valley, at least four miles from the cabin.

He pulled back his hood for a moment and studied the air above the banks for as long as his eyes could stand the exposure. The wind was blowing tangentially across the river, probably a point or two south of southwest. Depending on when the wind had shifted, he was probably closer to the center of the flats than the valley or the seashore. Which was not much help—the flatlands between sea and valley were wide, and it was impossible to make out landmarks.

He closed his eyes, letting them freeze shut again. The relative comfort he had in the riverbed fought with his impulse to do something, move somewhere. He could strike straight across the river and up the other bank, fighting the snow and helping the dogs. But then what? If he kept the wind at his back—the easiest way to travel—he would probably run head on into the side of the mountains that jutted out into the flatland. And this definitely was not mountain-climbing weather. Or he could estimate his position and cut back southeast, going across country in what he hoped was the direction of the cabin, keeping the wind on his right cheek as a guide. That option had the enticement of the warm cabin and hot food . . . if he could find the cabin in zero visibility. The dogs would be no help. They would approach the cabin from upwind and could easily miss the scent of home. And if they missed the cabin, they would end up out on the sea ice. Not good at all. A storm this fierce would have the ice snapping and heaving under the pressure of distant, wind-driven swells. This might even be one of the winter storms that broke up and cleared out all but a thin jut of land-fast sea ice. The fjord and ocean quickly froze over again, but that was small comfort to a man caught in the breakup.

Pulling the parka further over his face, he considered the possibility of following the river down to the sea and then hugging the coastline back to the Main Cabin peninsula. A long,

Snow cave

uncertain trail. He could feel the temperature dropping again. No more wet snow fell. The coming intense cold would sap his strength; sooner or later, he would begin to slow down and finally stop. And if the ice started to break up, the coastline would be an unpleasant place to be. Better to stay here than to push on until the storm robbed him of all but the desire to curl up out of the wind and sleep.

Sleep appealed to him even now, a danger signal. Without companionship, the constant reminder of his own frailty in the pinched and ice-streaked face of another, he had to be alert to his own physical limits. No one to wake him except himself.

The unmistakable seductiveness of the idea of sleep brought him grumbling to his feet. Muttering about the inevitability of it all, he stamped his feet to restore circulation. A few painful passes over his raw eyelids restored a little sight.

He groped in his pocket for a flashlight and on the sled for a shovel. As he clicked on the light, wind shouted across the banks, sending a cascade of crystalline flakes pouring into the riverbed. The temperature was falling perceptibly, and the wind was honing soft flakes into tiny razors. Blizzard coming on. With thousands of tons of new snow on the ground, the wind alone would be as crippling and blinding as the snow squall. Worse, the chill factor increased with the wind. The sooner he dug a snow cave and got into its shelter, the better chance he would have of staying warm, or at least unfrozen.

He quickly found what he needed in the yellow cone of light the flash gave him. Earlier winds had spilled a long, sloping snowbank down a notch in the riverbank. The snow was at least 9 feet deep, even discounting the new snow that had piled up. He set to work clearing off the loose new snow. When he was down to the hard-packed snow, he made a 3-foot-wide tunnel, working straight back toward the riverbank. He scored the hard-packed snow with the edge of the shovel and lifted it out in building blocks until he had tunneled 3 feet into the snowbank. At the end of the tunnel he made a chamber about 2 yards long, 1 yard wide, and slightly over 1 yard high.

As he worked, he felt hands and cheeks and feet burn with returning warmth. The little cave caught and held the heat from his own body, warming him further.

When finished, the chamber was adequate, though hardly spacious. He arranged the snow blocks into walls on either side of the opening, ensuring that the tunnel would not crumble under the wind. An hour after he began, the snow cave was complete except for hanging his nylon tent as a door.

When he backed out of his shelter, the wind was howling even between the riverbanks. The air was filled with sharp, tiny snow crystals hurled by a dry wind. Breathing became an icy hazard. Head lowered, mittened hand over nose and mouth, he checked the huskies. They did not so much as flick an ear at his attentions. The team was lined up beneath what miserable shelter the riverbank offered, tails over noses, backs to the wind, bodies rapidly disappearing under the drifting snow. In a few minutes they would be as warm as Ivar in his tiny snow cave—if not warmer.

He fumbled on the sled until he had freed his sleeping bag and stove. He hauled them into the cave, then returned for the folded pup tent, which he draped over the doorway and pegged into the snow walls. The nylon creaked with cold, but as it warmed it would make a reasonable windbreak. He could have set the tent up outside and saved himself the trouble of building a snow cave, but he would have ended up miserably cold. Nylon lacked the insulating capabilities of snow.

Inside the cave, out of the wind and cutting snow, he began to relax. The cave's temperature, although close to the zero mark, was 20 degrees warmer than outside, and his presence would raise it even more. The cave was dark, but so was the rest of the world. He worked by feel, spreading the sleeping bag and setting up the stove. In the flaring orange light of a match, he checked the cave for cracks, then lit the little primus stove. Its alcohol flame cast diffuse cerulean shadows as he gathered a small panful of snow which he put on top of the burner.

In a few minutes the snow melted to a quarter of its solid volume. He drank eagerly. As the tepid liquid spread through him, he scooped up another panful of snow. He could have melted the snow in his mouth, but that made about as much sense as running naked through a blizzard. He was far too cold to spare the body warmth required to turn snow into water; that was the stove's function.

He drank again, listening to the wind. Its groans and mutterings had shifted up the scale, more shrill, more sustained. It sounded as though he would be here for awhile. He brushed the snow off his clothes, slipped his ski boots off and crawled into the down sleeping bag to wait. Within minutes he felt himself warming as the down bag caught and held and reflected back his body heat, creating a near-tropical pocket of air next to his body. As feeling returned to his toes, he groaned with a mixture of pain and pleasure. Then he went through a period of shivering as his body readjusted from bone-deep chill. When the shivering passed, he felt almost human again.

The tiny stove still burned near the foot of his bag, melting the last pan of drinking water. He swallowed the water and blew the flame out. He did not know how long the storm would maroon him. He would have to hoard his small supply of fuel. As he shifted in the bag, he heard a faint noise in a pause between bursts of wind. The whine came again, then faded pathetically under a shrill wind howl.

Naika.

He pulled aside the tent cloth and saw her just outside the door of the cave. She had been curled up husky-style, but the movement of the cloth brought her head up. In the pale dark, he saw her tail quiver tentatively. Although the Arctic cold had called on ancestral canine genes, resulting in a 6-inch-long winter coat, Naika preferred to stay inside cabins and caves. She reminded him of that fact every chance she got. Not that he minded. If he had not been so thickheaded with cold, he would have invited her in sooner.

He set the stove aside and pulled back the door flap. Naika sprang through the open door and crowded into the cave beside him. As he pegged the flap shut again, he was rewarded for his kindness with a lick from a warm tongue. When he stretched out again, she flopped on the end of his sleeping bag, groaned happily and curled up. Her warmth seeped down through the bag to his feet.

He treated himself to regular glances at the luminous dial of his watch. The moving hands were tangible signs that minutes did indeed add up to hours, and that hours passed slowly, but they did pass. The storm outside did not pass. The sliding wind made eerie songs that both grated at and dulled his mind. Inside the mummy bag, with the radiating dog in the small dark womb of the cave, he was as warm and comfortable as the circumstances allowed.

Shortly after eight, about the time he should have been arriving at Main Cabin for dinner, his stomach began growling. He thought about the chocolate bars in the zipper pocket of his parka, but he made no move to collect them. The chocolate was for an emergency, and this hardly qualified. He ignored his stomach, as he had and would continue to ignore the claustrophobia and restlessness that niggled at the bottom of his mind.

Hunger returned in the small hours of morning. He rolled a cigarette. As he struck the match, he held it above his head, again surveying the snow cave. The interior warmth and exterior cold had struck a balance; a crust of ice glistened on the walls and ceiling of the cave, strengthening the structure. With the shovel handle, he poked a hole through the ice, venting the cave. The door was still snug. Drifts had built outside the flap, bulging the tight cloth and holding it down.

Satisfied that the cave would remain tight, he lit his cigarette, inhaled deeply, exhaled. The smoke curled out with his misty breath toward Naika. She had lifted her head to look at the glowing ember of light, and the smoke settled around her, producing a sneeze as it irritated her long nose. With a look of disgust, she put her nose under her tail again and sighed deeply. He laughed silently but made sure that future smoke missed her.

Their two bodies had warmed the air within the snow cave significantly. He could sit half out of his bag, his back braced against the hardened snow wall. As he smoked, he tasted each drag on the cigarette carefully, hoping his stomach would mistake flavor for nutrition. Tobacco was just the first of several ruses he used. Hornsund had taught him that hunger was relative. The gnawing of his stomach was often most insistent when his need for food was minor; he could appease his stomach with smoke or a handful of snow. The later stages of hunger were less uncomfortable—and more serious. A not unpleasant lightheadedness, an insidious lassitude that encouraged a dreamlike indifference to anything but sleep. That was the dangerous stage of hunger, when his body lacked calories to burn against the fierce cold. In the Arctic, he would freeze to death long before he starved.

He had been hungry many times, so hungry that his stomach stopped hurting and the icy world became warm and out of focus. In his second year of trapping, he had stayed at Bird Mountain working until the old lean-to was a snug cabin. He discovered a hot spring up behind the cabin and thought he had solved the problem of drinking water. No more collecting and stacking glacier ice for him. Just dip the bucket in and carry it back to the cabin. After awhile, he no longer noticed the sulphur smell.

He stayed at Bird Mountain on and off through the winter and drank the hot spring water. Even in the deepest cold, he only had to chop through a few inches of surface ice. About three weeks before dawn, his gums became tender, then sore. He had been eating well—he knew the danger of scurvy—and he assumed the soreness was temporary. It was not.

He hunted bear until April, when his gums began to bleed. He could see in the mirror that his teeth were crusted with some sort of deposit, but he could not scrape it off. A few teeth felt loose. Eating anything more solid than oatmeal was a chore. He knew he needed a doctor, but the nearest one was in Longyearbyen, nearly 130 miles by airplane. The distance on skis was another matter. It would depend on how lucky he was at picking smooth glaciers and inland mountain passes; there were no nicely marked trails. The coastline route was out—at least double the inland distance.

He added about 40 percent to the map distance inland. The dogs were in good shape, hard and strong from long runs up and down the fjord. If he did not load the sled too heavily with food, they should be able to average 40 miles a day. Long days, of course, eighteen hours at a stretch. If the weather held, he should be in Longyearbyen in five days.

He left from Main Cabin on a very cold spring day. The snow was like stone, and the huskies ran well. Once up on top of Hans Glacier, directly behind Main Cabin, he turned the team straight north, heading up the empty interior of the island toward Bellsund Fjord, 80 miles away. He knew that there were abandoned trappers' cabins there on the western edge of the bay.

For five hours the dogs ran up Hans Glacier's slope, away from the seashore. They made very good time on that first up-hill run, until they came to an area where other glaciers joined Hans. The ice was torn by conflicting forces, shattered into jagged piles and sudden cliffs. He had to rope the dogs one by one up ice walls. The huskies hated it. They progressed less than 400 yards in three hours.

And then the weather fell apart.

The clouds came down and the wind came up. Clouds and glacier met, making a dense ice fog. After an hour, Ivar could not even see his huskies. The fog and flying snow erased his carefully laid mental trail. Without landmarks, he was reduced to heading north and hoping for a break in the weather.

He was soon lost. A compass was unreliable so close to the North Pole. When the land continued to rise, he knew he was too far east, heading into the mountains. He turned the team northwest, trying to head down and away from the mountains, and came within a few feet of leading the dogs over a cliff. He backed up very carefully, turned the team, and headed over what he thought was his back trail. It was not. He knew the futility of floundering around; he stopped the team and decided to camp until the fog lifted.

After he fed the dogs, he tried to build a snow cave, but the snow was too hard for anything less than an ax. He fought the tent in the wind, then crawled inside and cooked up a pan of soup, all he could easily get past his gums. In spite of cold and hunger, he fell asleep quickly.

He woke up shivering. Drifting snow had piled up in front of the tent flap, wind still howled and there were no shadows. He knew without moving that the ice fog had not lifted, but he cracked the tent flap anyway. The dogs were restless, shifting uneasily on the ground and then standing and moving a few inches one way or the other, searching for a more comfortable spot. It was one of the few times he had seen the huskies too miserably cold to sleep.

Ivar was no better off. He lay in the sleeping bag, shifting like the dogs every few minutes to warm a different part of his body. He endured for twelve hours, listening to the wind and trying not to think. Finally the wind died a bit. Ice fog still covered the land, but he was too cold to wait any longer.

They left in a rush. The huskies were silent, ghostly. Their coats were filled with wind-driven ice crystals. Only their solid puffs of breath distinguished them from the snow they loped over. Gradually the fog thinned enough so that Ivar could see cliffs before he had one foot over the edge. He moved carefully anyway, feeling his way through the fog, hoping that the small glacier they were on would lead to the bigger, smoother glacier that would take them north. He felt the steep rise of mountains to his right, sensed the massive glacier further down, silent and white and ancient between ice-polished cliffs. Somehow he had to find a way down to the big valley glacier.

When he rested the dogs he studied the map, trying to match contour lines with the stone mountains looming in the fog. At first he thought that the fog was his only problem; then he realized that he was lost.

The next hours were all the same, groping through a frigid, colorless world, choosing paths with more hope than certainty. Ivar saw, or sensed, mountains on both sides, blank rock walls where a wide glacier should be. He stopped the dogs and studied the map again. Unless he was irrevocably lost, there was only one place he could be. Still too far east, on a small glacier leading to a ragged, impossible pass between two mountain ranges.

Ivar turned the team around and angled south-southwest, hoping to find a small glacier that would take him to the huge glacier that emptied into Bellsund Fjord.

The team moved across and then down a long sloping glacier that Ivar thought might be Tverrbreen, less than 20 miles from Bellsund. The glacier quickly became impassable, a mass of crevasses hidden beneath snow that was not hard enough to support man and sled and dogs.

Ivar followed his own back trail off the glacier, then turned south again, trying not to think of time and strength and bleeding gums. Further south, he turned the team onto another glacier. Impassable. He retreated, turned south again. The third glacier was a welcome surprise; instead of a splintered pile of ice, Hogstebreen turned out to be a nicely rumpled ramp leading down to the big valley glacier.

The team broke through the fog so suddenly that Ivar was stunned by flooding, hard-edged light. The valley glacier was a wide white highway. The tops of the mountains on either side were still blind with clouds, and a few feet above his head the blank fog reached down. The dogs flattened out, pulling him down and away from the murk.

The team held a fast pace for three more hours, covering as much ground as they had in the last two days. Finally Ivar stopped the team, made camp, fed the dogs, and attacked his lukewarm soup and half-melted cheese. He slept a long time, time he could not afford. Each dog should be getting 4 to 6 pounds of seal each day for the work they were doing, but they had been getting little more than 3 pounds apiece. And that was almost gone. When Ivar reached the seacoast again, there would be a chance to take seal or ptarmigan. But not up here;

the inland region was sterile. He had seen nothing but husky tracks since he had left Main Cabin.

The next day Ivar made 25 miles, down the place where Recherche Glacier met Bellsund Fjord. From high up on the glacier, he had seen a strip of dark blue in the distance. It was either open water or sky meeting ice. He hoped it was only the horizon. If Bellsund were not frozen solid, he would have a difficult, dangerous crossing ahead.

Ivar kept to the western edge of the glacier, toward the old cabins along a bay in the fjord. The cabin he chose was even smaller than Bird Mountain, but it was better than a tent; anything was better than a tent at 30 below with a hard wind blowing. As he fed the dogs and warmed soup, a storm closed in. It was another day before he could go outside, up on the mountain behind the cabin, to hunt for ptarmigan. He fed the dogs a bird apiece, not nearly enough, and saved the rest for the next day.

When he woke up, the clouds were low and racing. He hoped to cut straight across Bellsund Fjord before turning east and heading back along the northern shore of the fjord toward the valleys and glaciers that would finally lead him to Longyearbyen.

He soon discovered that the blue line was water. Wind and storm and tides had opened wide leads through the fjord ice. He would have to go further east, where Bellsund divided into two smaller fjords. On the map, the three fjords looked like a thick, ragged Y lying on its side. The northern arm was Van Mijen Fjord, the southern was Van Keulen. To reach Van Keulen, he would have to go south and east. back up the bay he had come down two days ago, then north across Van Keulen's mouth.

Ivar turned the team, backtracked, then went north across Van Keulen. The ice was solid, snow-covered, and often smooth.

They made good time toward the stone massifs that split Bell-sund in two.

Ivar let the team rest while he studied the ice and open water he must somehow cross. He knew there was a large, deserted cabin across Van Mijen, close to the point where Bell-sund and Van Mijen Fjords joined. He wanted to be in that cabin before the clouds became another storm.

Ahead and to his left he could see a long, narrow island that lay crosswise in Van Mijen's mouth. The island was the source of his ice problems. It forced the sea into channels barely 500 yards wide. Tidal surges churned through, sweeping ice out of the narrow openings on either shore of the fjord. Ivar realized he had to go further east, further away from the island.

After several hours, he turned the team out onto the ice. He lost track of the time as he advanced, backtracked, chose new directions in a zigzagging passage across shifting, groaning ice floes. When the team finally made it across and found the cabin, Ivar was shivering with cold and hunger. He fed himself and the dogs the last of the ptarmigan. As he slept, another storm closed in.

It was two days before Ivar and the team could leave. When the storm lifted, he harnessed the huskies and headed northeast, up a broad snow-filled valley. An hour later the huskies scented reindeer. Hungry huskies were deaf to any suggestion that they should ignore a potential meal. They were lean and drawn, more wolf than dog, and they ran like wolves after the herd. Ivar hung onto the towrope, grateful that the reindeer were heading north.

It was a long, uphill chase.

When the team finally closed within range, he unslung his rifle. He picked out a young bull, waited for a smooth stretch of ground and fired. The first shot brought the bull down and a second shot finished him.

Ivar yelled at the dogs to stop, but they were wild from the chase. He dug in sideways with his skis, plowing snow and yelling. Finally the huskies stopped, realizing that the chase was over. Blood was bright on the snow, the smell of blood filled the air, the team was ravenous. He had to work quickly or there would be a savage snarl of huskies fighting each other for the kill.

He kicked off his skis and ran to the dead reindeer. As he sliced off hunks of meat, he fired them at the team. The huskies gulped, snarling. When the snarls finally stopped, he cut himself a piece of tender filet. Minced up, with bits of liver and fat, the filet would replace weakness with strength.

While his meal cooked in snow water over the primus stove, Ivar cut chunks off the carcass and set them out in the snow to freeze. He felt no remorse about the absolutely illegal meal stretching his huskies' bellies and bubbling on his little stove. They had been two days without food, in intense cold. They had at least two more days of cold and effort before Longyearbyen. He might have felt guilty if that were the last reindeer on earth, but he would have shot it just the same.

Ivar sipped slowly at the rich mixture of meat and fat and water, ignoring his gums and the taste of his own blood blending with the meal. When he was finished, he made a quick camp and slept.

When he awoke, the last clouds were gone. As the huskies trotted up the wide valley, he looked back toward the dead reindeer lying on a frozen blanket of blood and understood the meaning of an old Eskimo saying: A man has never known hunger until he has eaten with wolves.

The last days of the trip went smoothly. No more storms, ample food for the dogs, easy trails and passes. He smelled Longyearbyen hours before he saw its coal smoke rising ahead. When he went to the clinic, a doctor and a dentist examined him. They both agreed that except for his mouth and a pronounced lack of fat, he was healthy. Then they disagreed. The doctor thought scurvy was Ivar's problem. The dentist blamed alkali deposits from the Bird Mountain hot spring. The dentist scraped Ivar's teeth and the doctor pumped him full of vitamins. They both agreed he should spend a week or two doing nothing more strenuous than eating and sleeping.

He followed their orders for almost four days before restlessness got the better of him. His gums had stopped bleeding, he could chew again and he had put on several pounds. He was having trouble adjusting to other people. If there was more than one person in the room, it was easier not to say anything. What he wanted was to be back home in Hornsund. Alone.

Ivar went to the commissary and stocked up on vitamins and supplies for the trip home. The huskies were as eager to leave as he was—they despised kennel fences. They left Longyearbyen late that evening. The trip home was easy and beautiful. Blue sky and endless sun, hard snow and smooth crossings. They reached Main Cabin in four days, the best time he had ever made anywhere.

Going home.

Ivar listened to the wind, still violent. He checked his watch. Ten hours gone while he dreamed so as to close out the storm and open up the tiny snow cave. He sat up in the sleeping bag, upsetting Naika, and pulled the door flap aside. Snow still boiled through the air. He replaced the flap, slid down into the bag and slept.

When he awoke, snow still raced outside. He melted a pan of snow, rolled a cigarette and waited, fighting the restlessness that demanded he be up and out of the tight dark cave.

I could have sat out this storm in Cabin Bay, drinking and

*playing chess. But I'd have been lousy company. It's the god-
damned dark that gets me. I can't sit still after awhile. Maybe
getting good and hungry will teach me a lesson.*

Grumbling to himself, he put out the cigarette and tried
to sleep again. When he came out of the half-sleeping, half-
waking trance induced by cold and dark and isolation, he
pulled the flap aside. Snow still blew, but most of the ice flakes
were no more than a foot or two off the ground. The huskies
were completely drifted over, small mounds in the smooth
river bottom.

When Ivar scraped snow into the pan, Svarten stirred. The
big husky stood and shook the snow from his fur, a signal that
the storm was indeed lifting.

Ivar leaned back into the cave, rousted Naika and shagged
her out into the cold. Then he set up the primus to melt the
pan of snow. He drank several pans of lukewarm water, ignoring his rumbling, complaining stomach. Two days without food
was nothing in the middle of winter. He still had a layer of fat
beneath his skin. By the end of spring, when the cold was
deepest and he was working eighteen hours out of twenty-four,
his fat would vanish and a day without food would be a hardship. He would eat twice as much and lose 20 pounds. In the
Arctic, every animal burned huge quantities of food just to
stay warm. Winter fat was not the mark of a glutton, but of a
survivor.

He packed quickly in the lightless cave, trying to defeat
the cold by constant movement. The stove was like ice, though
minutes ago it would have burned incautious fingers. By the
time he rolled the sleeping bag his fingers were numb. He
pulled on his mittens and took down and rolled the tent. As he
crawled out the opening, he automatically picked up his rifle.
Most bears denned up during a big storm, but a few prowled
hurricanes as easily as he skied a downhill glacier.

He stood and strained into the dark. His eyes saw nothing but a low slaty swirl of snow, his ears heard nothing but the wind, his unnamed senses felt only the immense isolation of Arctic night. He shouldered his rifle, grabbed the shovel and began digging the sled out. As he worked, the dogs roused themselves and stood in the traces.

After ten minutes of searching, Ivar helped the dogs pull the sled up a low spot he had found in the riverbank. On the flats the snow blew in knee-high curls. Hollows were drifted over in loose snow, changing the land. But even as he looked, he knew that the drifts were shifting and shrinking and packing under the relentless wind. In the hazy starlight he saw mountains silhouetted and immediately knew where he was. He found a trail down to the seashore and then followed the shore around to his cabin.

What he could see of the fjord was mottled black and gray, and he smelled damp salt spray in the air. As he had half expected, the storm had broken up and carried away the thick sea ice while he was warm and safe in his snow cave. But like the land, the sea would soon return to rigid winter normal. The awesome storms that could smash thousands of square miles of ice always were equaled by the silent, freezing power of Arctic night.

The last leg of the trip took three hours. He was thoroughly cold when he reached the cabin, but that was thoroughly normal. He fed the dogs, talking to them over the minor-key moan of the wind. When they finished eating, he knelt beside each one of them, rumpling their fur, assuring himself that there were no masked casualties from the fall down the riverbank. He enjoyed the slippery-rough textures of fur between his fingers, the slide from outer cold to insulated warmth. And the huskies enjoyed his attentions, particularly Svarten, who always seemed disappointed that Ivar was not going to stay and sleep under a cozy snowdrift with the team.

Satisfied that the dogs were well, Ivar went to the cabin. He took a broom and swept the hoarfrost off ceiling and walls and floors before he fired the stove. To appease his growling stomach, he set about making a big, calorie-rich meal. Goose and creamy gravy, potatoes and vegetables and fruit, bread thick with jam and butter. Then coffee, steaming with warmth and sugar and Scotch.

When he could eat no more, he read by the heavy gold light of the kerosene lamp. After the cramped snow cave, the cabin was a palace of exotic delights. When his eyes blurred, he warmed up the radio, playing his guitar and singing along with the songs he knew, listening carefully to the ones he did not know.

And when his eyes and fingers and voice were tired, he sat in front of the fire, sipping Scotch until his mind was ready for sleep.

In the morning he resumed his trapline rounds, beginning with the coastline traps, which had taken the brunt of the storm. It was dark and cold and desolate work, digging out traps that were drifted full or tripped by the wind, lifting and replacing 80 pounds of rock at each trap. In the long, lightless days, there were treasured moments of clear skies and silver moon, but the clouds always returned, blotting out light. When he was too tired to lift more rocks, but not tired enough to sleep, he worked with his guitar, creating new songs.

But loneliness still swept over him, especially when he lay in bed trying to sleep. When the feeling of isolation threatened to suffocate him, he switched on a flashlight and played it over the walls and ceiling of the cabin. Pinup girls and photographs of friends stared back at him. Most of the time the pictures came alive as his mind played with past memories, present dreams, future possibilities. He could lie for hours composing, changing, rejecting, polishing his dreams like an artist with a three-dimensional canvas.

Yet this night, five nights after Christmas, the pictures remained merely pictures, flat and dead. He clicked off the flashlight and tried to sleep, telling himself over and over that the Arctic night was half gone.

While he slept, a huge wind swept down the fjord, scouring away the snow from the front entrance of the cabin. The next hard wind would probably cover it up again, and he would have to dig yet another snow tunnel exit, but he enjoyed the bare doorstep anyway.

The wind kept him inside the cabin, working over fox pelts, scraping, turning, stretching until his fingers grew clumsy and his eyes ached. As he put the last pelt on the stretcher frame, he heard the huskies snarling above the dying wind. He pulled on his parka, grabbed the rifle out of the storage room and went cautiously outside. Although he had seen the wide, long pugmarks of bear as he worked the traplines, he had yet to see a bear. But when he went up to the dogs, they were already curling up again. Either the bear had fled or had been too far off to be of much interest.

He checked the dogs, though he had few worries about their safety. Their chains were long, their teeth sharp; any bear that tried to take on the pack would have a real fight. In four years, he had never had a husky injured by a polar bear.

Nevertheless, he kept his rifle close at hand, always, even though he was not eager to hunt in darkness. He wanted each one of his allotted ten bears to be prime male pelts, but he would not hesitate to kill a bear, any bear, if he or the dogs were in danger.

After a last look around, he went to the side of the cabin

and removed the window shutter. With the wind almost gone, he could once again sit and stare outside during his meals. Not that he could see much, but the cabin seemed less like a prison with the window uncovered.

He went back inside the cabin, trying not to think about time and the crawling progress of night. Tomorrow, for much of the world, a new year would begin. But not for him; his years were marked out by unyielding Arctic cycles. New Year's Day came in the second week of February, when the blood-red disk of the sun first breached the horizon.

Inside the living area, he removed his parka and went to work on ptarmigan rather than foxes. With small, deft motions he skinned two birds, basted them with butter and herbs and put them into the oven. He kicked off his boots, hesitated, then peeled off his heavy wool sweater. With an unconscious sigh, he settled back in a chair with a glass of Scotch, listening to the fire and the glacial music of compressed ice thawing in his drink.

As the Scotch drained away the tension of darkness, the warm fire and gentle lamplight made him sleepy. He pulled himself out of the chair long enough to baste the roasting birds, then sat down at the table and drowsed again.

He was lifted out of half sleep by a faint sound along the wall behind him. At first he thought it was Naika, then knew it could not be; her head was a heavy warmth on his stocking feet. Adrenaline swept away his stupor as he recognized the *snuffle, snuffle* of a polar bear scouting the wall of the cabin. The bear must have approached from downwind, for the huskies had not given alarm. Naika rumbled, then fell silent at a gesture from him. He reached under the table and pressed her head to the floor, a command not to move.

Quietly, he set the Scotch on the table and went to the window. In the golden rectangle of lamplight, he caught a glimpse of the bear as it ambled down the side of the cabin. The rump was heavy and broad—either a very large female or a medium-sized male. He looked at the tracks, dark shadow depressions in the iron-hard snow, then he blew out the lamp and let his eyes adjust to darkness. Waiting and listening. The bear had probably been drawn by the scent of roasting ptarmigan, but there was also a cache of seal meat on the roof. And the unsuspecting dogs, upwind of the bear.

Ivar moved across the cabin on noiseless stocking feet, his undershirt a vague white blur in the dark room. He gathered his rifle and reached the outer door just as the huskies went wild. He slapped the rifle bolt and checked the breech by feel. Loaded and ready. Forgetting that he was only half dressed, he went to the outer door, planning to surprise the bear from downwind just as the bear had surprised the dogs. Knowing that the yammering dogs would cover any sound he made, he pulled the door open.

The team had also covered bear sounds very nicely.

Even as his senses registered the bear rising out of the darkness right in front of him, the rifle snapped up and the sound of two quick shots drowned out the dogs. The bear somersaulted backward and rolled down and out of sight.

He kicked the door shut and jacked a third round into the rifle chamber. Then he stood and listened, knowing that a wounded bear would make more noise than any eight teams. Two shots at point-blank range into the base of the neck should have killed the bear, but he was not going to bet his life on it. He had used up enough luck for one night.

No sounds except the din of the huskies straining at the ends of their chains to get at the bear. He kept on waiting and hoping that the bullets had done their work, that he would not have to go out and track a wounded bear in utter darkness.

Suddenly the night exploded into growls and massive roars

and the repeated *slam-slam* of great hooked paws against the wall of the cabin. Splintering-tearing sounds as tar paper and logs gave under the immense power of an enraged polar bear.

He did not stop to wonder how a bear that should have had a broken neck could be so terrifyingly alive. The longer he lived in the Arctic, the more he respected the white bear's incredible strength and savagery. He knew a full-grown bear was quite capable of reducing the cabin to kindling.

He waited for a moment, waited to see if the mauling would abate, but it grew in intensity. He could either stay put until the trembling wall beside him gave way, or he could go outside and face the bear.

He slipped across the darkened entryway and into the storeroom. There was a trapdoor in the ceiling, an emergency exit after heavy storms. He climbed the short ladder quickly. With the rifle barrel, he lifted the square trap and pushed it back. Rifle at the ready, he silently pulled himself out on the roof. It was like stepping into an ice cube, but he did not notice the cold. As he stood up, the sounds of the attack stopped. Maybe the bear had finally died.

He scanned the roof, then crept on hands and knees toward the corner that the bear had attacked. Cautiously, finger curled around the trigger, he eased his eyes over the edge of the roof, expecting to see the wounded bear directly beneath him.

Empty snow.

His eyes swept the area to the limits of his night vision. Nothing.

He eased a few feet to his right, looking down the other side of the cabin. There, immediately to his right and at a spot that would have been just out of sight from the entryway door, lay the bear, unmoving. He relaxed. There would be no more trouble from that bear. But it must have been extraordinarily powerful to attack the cabin like that with its dying strength.

A small stealthy sound behind him sent his back hairs up on end. He spun on his knees in time to see the head and shoulders of a white bear rise above the edge of the roof. At Ivar's movement, the bear knew the stalk was over. It leaped for the roof in a single surge of white power.

Ivar's reflexes took over, triggering a shot at the same instant the bear leaped. The shot caught the bear in the chest. The huge animal hung for a moment, defying gravity. A second shot tipped the balance. The bear tumbled backward in slow motion, landing on the drifts at the back of the cabin with a muffled thump. The ear-numbing roars of bear and rifle were absorbed by darkness, leaving only a residue of sound from the frenzied huskies.

He released his breath in one long, toneless whistle, took a slow breath of cold air and held it, tasting it, savoring it, aware of all its icy textures. Mechanically he slapped the bolt of the rifle, flipping the cartridge out. It rang musically on the icy roof, then rolled down and disappeared over the edge, falling noiselessly into the snow. He rammed a new cartridge home before he advanced to look over the roof where the attacking bear had disappeared.

It lay a few feet below the edge of the roof, on a snowdrift that had piled up within a yard of the eave. He waited for several long moments, straining into the darkness for any sign of movement. There was none.

Satisfied that the animal would not resume its attack, he retraced his steps across the roof. The first bear lay exactly as he had seen it. It was as large as the one that had so nearly caught him on the roof, or slightly larger. Except for females with cubs—and either bear looked too large to be a cub—it was extraordinary to find bears pairing and traveling together. Even in mating season, alliances were usually brief and savage. It would be interesting to solve the mystery.

He suddenly realized that he was intensely cold. His nearly bare feet had lost all sensation; his right hand, curled around rifle stock and trigger, was immovable.

He hobbled across the roof toward the trapdoor. By hooking his left arm through the ladder rungs, he prevented a headlong descent. By the time he reached the floor he was shivering violently. He stowed the rifle in its rack and made his way into the living quarters, where the heat of the stove rolled over him. Soon the stove and the shivering restored his temperature to near normal. He pulled his clothes on, retrieved the rifle and went outside for a more thorough inspection of the two bears.

As he emerged from the cabin, the team was still snarling and huffing and growling furiously. A few shouts and a string of curses restored silence. He needed quiet to think—and to hear bears.

He snapped on the flashlight and clamped it over the rifle barrel with his left hand; whatever moved within that cone of light would automatically be a target. As he approached the first bear, he saw that it was young. Fur of purest white, muzzle soft with short white hairs, no scars. Closer examination showed that the bear was average-sized, perhaps a little larger, and male. He checked for reflexes with the tip of the rifle barrel against the bear's eye, but there was no movement. The bear was definitely dead.

Moving silently around the cabin, he compared the position of the second bear with his rooftop memories. No change, no reflex from rifle barrel on unprotected eye. Very dead.

The second bear was female, old. Almost all of her muzzle was black and callused, the white hairs worn off from years of scraping against snow and ice. A truly ancient matron. Improbable as it seemed, the other must have been her cub, staying with her long after the usual two years. That would explain the blind savagery of her attack. A female with a cub, even a fully grown cub, was always more dangerous than an adult male.

In the moving cone of light, he assessed the old bear's pelt. It was showing signs of age, faint yellowing around the shoulders, worn fur between the pads of her feet. He guessed that the other bear would have been her last cub, no matter how many more seasons she might have lived. But she was large; her body fur was thick, shiny and had no obvious scars.

He knelt beside her and touched the aged muzzle.

You had no choice, but I had no choice either.

He turned off the flashlight and stood slowly, suddenly very tired. Tomorrow he would hitch up the team and drag the bears to the snow pit where the first bear of the winter lay. For tonight, he could protect the two bears from scavengers roaming the hungry night.

Before going back to the cabin, he checked the huskies, soothing them and making sure their frenzy had not tangled their chains. When he opened the living-room door, Naika's low whine reminded him that she was waiting to be released from his command to stay. At his signal she scrambled out from under the table, nearly knocking over a chair. He fended her off as he pulled the two ptarmigan out of the oven. Their meat was dry, tough from overcooking, and he ate every bit with relish. As he was clearing the table, he glanced at the clock on the shelf above the sink. Five minutes past midnight, January 1.

New Year's was followed by three weeks of wind and storm, trapline work and intense restlessness. The end of the long Arctic night was near, but the fact did not comfort him. Light was hanging just below the southeast horizon, two weeks to dawn. Just fourteen days. Just eternity.

Because the end of darkness was so close, he had unconsciously loosened his control over his tightly held emotions. Now they were racing ahead of him like a runaway team, pulling him in every direction. Almost three months with no more light than rare, cloudless hours dotted with tiny stars, and rarest of all, a full moon in a clear sky. Pale moon, paler stars, tiny lamps and flashlights and fires. Not enough. Not nearly enough. Cold and black and alone on the edge of the world.

He struggled against his writhing loneliness, knowing that it would vanish with the first touch of sunlight. But it was a difficult battle. Main Cabin's amenities no longer held his interest. Radio, guitar, books, even Scotch bored him. His mood was savage. Each day he made a small ritual of striking a square off the calendar, telling himself that was one less piece of night to endure, one less day in hell. Two weeks left, then twelve days, then ten.

Each noon he stood outside, scanning the southeast horizon for the faintest chalky-gray promise of dawn. Each day he worried that the predawn time would be cloudy or stormy, that the promise would not be kept. One night he dreamed that the entire month of February was one interminable storm that hid day from him and drove him insane. He awoke, shivering in the cold and darkness.

When the countdown to light reached seven days, his restlessness won. The Main Cabin traplines had not yielded a single fox in ten days. The foxes were either smart or dead. He had no more skins to prepare except those of the three bears frozen beneath the snow. He could not skin a frozen carcass; the bears would have to wait for the sun to thaw them. He had cleaned the cabin twice in one day. Bread was baked for a month. Harness was shining and supple. Rifles had been cleaned until they gleamed like antique pewter. He had melted enough ice to take a bath and wash his clothes. There was simply nothing left to do but wait for dawn, and waiting for dawn was a sure way to come down with terminal cabin fever.

It was time to go to Bird Mountain.

The dogs, including Naika, would stay at Main Cabin. If he took the team and found that the sea ice was impassable, he would have to turn back; the inland route was too rugged for the team.

He hacked off a generous amount of seal, better than three days' food for each dog, and chained Naika with the team. The meat would be gulped or hoarded, depending on each dog's temperament. Either way, the dogs were good for up to a week of waiting without hardship.

With the dogs taken care of, he attended to his own needs. A small supply of food, in case the cabin's stores had been raided by a bear. Pup tent, sleeping bag, ammunition, two very sharp knives, matches, primus stove, fuel, tobacco bag, extra socks, three chocolate bars, flashlight and extra batteries. And the Mauser, of course.

Everything but the rifle and knives went into the backpack, with no room left over. He eased the pack on, flexed his shoulder muscles to settle the load and picked up the Mauser. Although the rifle weighed 14 pounds, he accepted its weight as automatically as he accepted the weight of his own body. After a last check of the dogs, he set out on skis for Bird Mountain.

For the first time in weeks, the sky was partly clear and the wind was merely a minor-key moan over the frozen land. Starlight reflected by snow gave him a visibility of 15 feet. Even though he knew it was too soon, he kept on looking ahead, hoping to spot at least a faint paling of predawn in the east. Once his heart leaped at a silver glow spreading above the mountains, but in the next second he realized it was only the moon. Yet even that slender crescent added a few feet of visibility to his tiny world.

He shuffled east, reminding himself with every other step that this was indeed a different piece of ice, a different trail, a different destination. Something new. But for all his self-lecturing, he felt like an ant on a treadmill. There were only so many ways ice could respond to wind and tide, and he had seen them all, too many times. Without light, certainty of progress was a matter of faith reinforced by experience.

From time to time he checked his compass, more out of boredom than real need. The contours of the snow-covered sea ice told him that he was still paralleling the twisting shoreline, still secure on the land-fast ice shelf that rose and dropped but rarely broke up under tidal stress. Right now, the thought of anything breaking or melting or changing was ludicrous—the sea ice was silent and endless, a frozen featureless eternity, ever and always, world without end, amen.

And the clouds had closed up again. No dawn preview today.

When he came across a jumbled area where last summer's icebergs had clumped and frozen, he was almost grateful. He poled right, then left, seeking a way to ski through, then decided it would be quicker to walk. He took off his skis and picked his way through the waist-high, lumpy mass. The rough stretch was just long enough to make him glad to put on the skis again.

In another mile, he found polar-bear sign. The tracks were faint in the hard snow, slight pad depressions topped by neat claw holes. The tracks led east, toward Bird Mountain.

He pulled off his right mitten and knelt by a broad pugmark. His finger traced the inside of the track. Only a light dusting of snow over it, but with the hard crust and rather light wind, it was difficult to judge how old the track was. Hours or days, no way to be sure. He unslung his rifle and scanned the lightless, jagged ice. Slowly, quietly, he followed the tracks, ears alert for any sound.

The trail led to a large dark stain over the snow. Nearby was a knee-high, shattered ice dome. He did not need light to know what had happened. The dome was the result of a seal's breath freezing above its breathing hole. Beneath the broken dome would be an inverted funnel leading down to the water, formed by the seal's body as it returned again and again through thickening ice to breathe.

The hole was iced over now, for the seal was dead. The bear had enlarged the small breathing hole to paw size, then waited for the seal to return. Eventually the seal had appeared, needing oxygen in order to continue its hunt for food beneath the frozen lid of the fjord. The kill had been quick. A massive white paw had descended with enough force to turn the seal's brains literally to jelly; then claws dug in for a sharp pull upward that yanked the fat seal out of the small hole. Between one second and the next, every bone in the seal's 200-pound body was crushed, eviscerating the carcass and stretching it far beyond its normal length.

Messy, but efficient.

He circled the area until he found bear tracks heading off to the northeast, then he returned to examine what was left of the ringed seal. The blubber had been stripped off the hide as neatly as if the bear had used a skinning knife. Not a scrap of the energy-rich fat remained. The flesh itself was pecked and gnawed, showing that ivory gulls and foxes had been at work scavenging the meat that the polar bear disdained. The kill was probably twelve hours old, the bear full and far away, the path

Bird Mountain Cabin, late winter

to Bird Mountain as safe as it ever was. Somewhere, not far away, the foxes and gulls were waiting for him to leave.

He stood and pulled his mitten back on, but left the rifle unslung, carrying it so that a quick movement of his right arm would bring the gun into firing position. It was an awkward way to travel, but he was used to it.

When he arrived at Bird Mountain Cabin, it showed the scars of winter, plus long scratches down the wall where a prowling bear had casually raked claws across tar paper. A recent wind had dislodged the spring cache of dog food from the roof. The seal lay uncovered in the snow near the doorway. Bear tracks were all around it; the seal hide had long gouges but was otherwise intact. Apparently the bear preferred its dinners warm.

He considered heaving the carcass back onto the roof, then decided not to. The next bear probably might not be so fussy. He would rather have bears gnawing on the seal than gnawing on the cabin, or him.

The inside of the cabin was dark, cold and coated with hoarfrost. He swept out the frost before he lit the fire. The 6-foot-square living room warmed quickly.

Ivar shrugged out of his parka and put the rifle in the entryway-storeroom. The stove's heat would not penetrate that far, and the rifle would be safe from repeated cycles of heat and cold that could leave a destructive condensation of water and ice in the firing mechanism. Though he invariably cleaned his rifles at least once a week, he knew that no amount of care could compensate for alternating between fire and ice.

He warmed his fingers by the stove until they were supple again. After he had eaten an indifferent dinner of stew and coffee, he put on his parka and went back to the storeroom. He pulled open the hinged panel in the outer door, looked out, saw nothing. He picked up a hammer and a can of nails from a nearby shelf and renailed the tar paper on the outside of the cabin and the insulation on the inside. Where wind and claws had torn the tar paper, frost had got underneath the insulation, forcing it away from the wall. Nothing serious, but worth repairing.

Inside again, he sat in the lamplight for a few minutes, studying the 6-by-6-foot living space for other projects, and finally decided on a small shelf below the window, on the wall beside the stove, opposite the bunk. It was the only section of wall that was not already in use for storage. A fine place for tobacco, Scotch, seasonings and whatever else would fit.

By the time the shelf was completed and completely full, he felt ready for sleep.

The next day he walked the Bird Mountain trapline, digging out and setting twenty traps. Even though he planned on staying only a few days, he might take a fox. A lot of work, probably for nothing, but he had a lot of time and a need to use his energy for something more constructive than waiting for the sun. At noon he rested, scanned the dark gray ceiling of clouds, and knew that no light would reach him today. He went back to work, lifting stones and traps and trying not to think.

When he returned to the cabin, the wind was picking up a little, just enough to make moaning noises through rocky passes and around cabin eaves.

The wind shifted from moans to occasional high cries, making Bird Mountain seem more isolated than before. He stood in the cabin doorway, letting the wind's icy fingers lift through his long hair, gauging as best he could the weather's temper. In spite of the wind's strength, it did not have the feel of storm about it. No razor ice crystals, no blinding-choking snow, no deep, sustained power. Just a routine Arctic wind scraping over the frozen fjord.

He shrugged into his parka and went out to check the window shutter. He tugged hard at it, making sure it was secure against anything but a determined bear.

Satisfied, he went back inside to prepare his evening meal. As he cooked and sipped Scotch, he was keenly aware of his isolation. Not even Naika's alert brown eyes for company, no team to warn of bears, few supplies if a long storm settled in. All for an unnecessary trip, a sop to his savage cabin fever. The realization of unnecessary risks made him uneasy. In previous years he would have taken greater chances without a second thought. Now he took chances, then told himself what a damned fool he was.

Shivering, he pulled his chair closer to the oil-barrel stove. In spite of his work, Bird Mountain was not as snug as Main Cabin. When the fire faded to embers, the room temperature would drop like a head-shot goose. Even now a skim of ice had formed on the water bucket; by morning the water would be as solid as stone.

Ivar finally gave up and crawled into the mummy bag on the bunk, which filled one entire wall of the cabin. In spite of the cold, he slid into the down bag wearing no more than his undershirt. Any more clothes and he would wind up uncomfortably warm. Any less, and the draft from the opening of the mummy bag would stiffen his neck and shoulders. He eeled deep into the bag, reached over his head, and tied the top as tightly as he could from the inside. His fingers, already numb with cold, fumbled. The result was a knot, but he did not bother to untangle it. It would be easier in the morning, when his fingers were warm.

The wind flexed around the cabin in a sustained roar that subsumed all other sounds. The fire, less than 3 feet away from his bed, warmed only the oil barrel. He slept restlessly for an hour or more.

Looking for a meal

The strident sounds of splintering wood, screeching nails and shattering glass brought Ivar instantly awake. Only a polar bear could demolish the heavily shuttered window so quickly. And with the window gone, all the rich food smells of the cabin would pour out, spurring the bear's hunger.

Ivar thrust his hands above his head, groping for the tie cord. As he tugged at the cord, he heard the delicate, filelike sound of bear claws brushing down the nylon skin of the mummy bag. It took him less than a second to remember the knot and realize he was trapped.

A heavy weight fell on his chest and the sound of claws became less delicate. The bear had reached across the room and was testing the curious, unfleshlike covering of the wriggling bag. Adrenaline swept through Ivar's body, releasing a wave of strength. His arms went rigid, then slammed out against the bag, once, twice, and the tough nylon split away from his driving fists.

He flattened himself on the bunk, trying to avoid the bear's probing paw as he peeled the sleeping bag off his body and kicked free. He started to sit up, but his head crashed into what felt like a rock. Even as he realized that the rock was the polar bear's lower jaw, he threw himself flat again and scooted down the bunk on his back.

The sudden blow and the equally sudden appearance of Ivar's white undershirt where the dark mummy bag had been caused the bear to pull back slightly. Ivar was so close to the animal's massive head that he saw the bear's eyes widen with surprise, smelled the mixture of carnivore breath and spilled Scotch from the shattered bottle on the new shelf, felt the quick rush of air as the bear cleared its nostrils of the astringent alcohol scent. The bear's withdrawal sent a second bottle of Scotch flying over the stove. The room reeked of steaming, stinging Scotch, and the wind poured snow through the open window.

When the bear sneezed, Ivar came off the bunk in a tumbling rush. His bare feet came down on a pile of broken glass. He felt cutting edges and heard his curses over the bear's snarls. He threw himself back on the bunk, yanked pieces of glass out of his foot and hit the floor at the far end of the bed.

The smell of blood encouraged the polar bear; its paw hissed by Ivar's body. Had he been standing, he would have been neatly gutted. He scrambled toward the door of the room without thinking, intent only on getting to his rifle in the entryway-storeroom before the bear got more than a long neck and a longer arm into the tiny cabin.

The bear pushed hard against the groaning window frame and swiped again, lower this time. Ivar heard the whistle of claws an inch above his head. He hugged the floor and squirmed on. Then there was silence broken only by the creak of the door as he pushed it open and crawled into the storeroom.

He noticed the silence but not the minus-20 cold of the outer room as he stood up. He lifted the rifle from its rack, pushed a round into the chamber and slipped to the outer door. He listened. Nothing. He held his breath. Still no sound. Slowly, he eased open the hinged panel in the upper half of the door.

The bear's head and neck burst through the opening. Ivar jumped back, narrowly avoiding the open mouth and lethal teeth. Two steps and he was flat against the closed living-room door. The bear's hot breath bathed his stomach. No room to swing the door open and escape back into the living room, not even room to bring the rifle to his shoulder. The small space seemed filled with claws and teeth.

He raised the rifle over his head, wrapped his left hand around the barrel, hooked his right thumb through the trigger and slammed the muzzle down on top of the bear's weaving

Ivory gull

very cold and tipped with ice. Another storm in the making.

Half an hour later, just before noon, he stopped and drank from the small canteen he carried inside his parka. The water was chilly but well above freezing. As he tucked the canteen away again, he glanced overhead. The stars were very pale, almost invisible. The clouds were mounds of dark gray wool. He looked automatically over his shoulder, southeast. He blinked, fought the impulse to rub his eyes, and stared. There, unmistakably, were the twin points of Hornsund Peak, silhouetted against the faintest wash of pale, pale blue light. As he watched, the horns sharpened, then faded again into darkness and clouds.

The afterimage glowed in his mind like a first kiss from a shy and lovely woman.

He leaned on his ski poles for a long moment, wondering if he had really seen that pale light, knowing he had, but hardly daring to believe. It had been so long since he had seen the mountains across the fjord that it was almost as though they existed only in his memory. But the mountains were real. He had seen them. The long night was ending.

He straightened above his ski poles and pushed over the fjord ice with easy, powerful strides.

Dawn

Ivar had been trapped at Main Cabin for four days. The storm that he sensed building had arrived from the west, a wild storm that made the sea ice shriek and blew countless tons of snow over the frozen land. Somewhere, high above the heaving ice and snow, predawn light breathed pale colors over the sky . . . but he could not see beyond his outstretched arm. He stood as he had so many times during the night, head poked out in the storm, praying for a break in the weather. At last he withdrew into the warm cabin and the warmer sleeping bag. He tried to tell himself that it really did not matter. Sooner or later the clouds would blow away, and when they did he would finally see the sun. His lecture had no effect; tomorrow was dawn and he ached to see the sunrise.

He woke up after a few hours and lay quietly, wondering what had awakened him. Then he realized that the wind was nearly gone. Except for a few residual groans from compressed sea ice, the night was silent. He smiled and fell asleep again, knowing that the day of dawn would be still and cold and clear.

In the six o'clock darkness, he took care to eat a good breakfast, for he knew he would not be back until dinner. As he ate he kept his eyes on the unshuttered window. Snow rose in a drift that crested just short of the glass. Above the snow, stars glittered in the obsidian sky.

When he was ready to leave, Naika leaped ahead of him to the outer door. He thumped her ribs gently and opened the door. She bounded through the drifts, breaking trail to the seal cache. He cut short his rounds with the huskies, taking time only to reassure Svarten that his day was coming.

Seven o'clock.

He skied toward the seashore leg of his circular trapline. While Naika waited at a discreet distance, he dug out and re-baited the traps brought down by the storm. He found no foxes. When the traps were open for business, he pushed on toward the flatlands traps without resting.

Ten o'clock.

With measured, rhythmic strides he worked his way toward Fox Valley. He knew he should get the trapline in working order as soon as possible, for the foxes would be prowling hungrily after the last storm. But he kept slowing, looking to the east, straining toward the first hint of dawn.

Eleven o'clock.

He worked his way up the sloping shoulder of the mountains at the east side of Fox Valley as far as he could go on skis, then he stopped and leaned on his ski poles. He glanced impatiently toward the east—and realized that dawn had begun while he climbed. Slowly draining darkness and substance out of the night, mountains had condensed around him. As he watched, the mountaintops just above him became clean black lines against a scoured pewter sky.

He kicked off his skis and climbed to meet the dawn.

Just before noon he reached the top of a bare, windswept ridge. He sat quietly on an icy rock, facing east. Overhead the sky was a gray satin sheet stretched by the wind. A pale-blue glow appeared, deepened, strengthened. The mountains became subtly textured black masses crowned by shifting pastel banners. Subtle pinks and lemon yellow, whispering blues and a promise of amber. The highest peaks radiated purple, flared to crimson and every dream of gold. Light flowed down mountain ridges in a silent rush of color.

The sun rose incandescent.

All beginnings, all hopes, all lives. So beautiful, so fierce. The burning center of life. . . .

He blinked, realized he was standing with his hat in hand, tears frozen on his cheeks. He pulled his hat into place and sat again, drinking the pouring colors. He looked at the mountains near and far, recalling cornices and peaks like old friends, expanding into the world that the sun had given back to him. That awesome rising disk, lavishing light on the white snow and stone mountain ridges, wastrel sun, spilling light and life over a frozen land.

As he sat motionlessly, the flow of colors paled. A tide of darkness lapped at the base of the mountains, then surged upward, leaving the peaks as island ridges of light. The sun was sliding down, a half disk, a fiery thread, gone. The half-hour day was over.

But each day the sun would climb higher, stay longer. In less than a month there would be twelve hours of sunlight. In April the sun would never set. Then the land would no longer be locked in ice and silence and waiting. Life would return in dizzying, thunderous rush.

The sun's gift would not be wasted.

Morning

The hard, cold, blue-edged light of the middle March sun lay across Hornsund, casting narrow shadows around shore rocks and huge splinters of broken sea ice off the Main Cabin coastline. Ivar and the team moved across the flatland shelf and down a narrow break through the ice barrier built by tides and slashing storm waves.

Snow squeaked cleanly beneath sled runners as the team trotted across the sea ice to the first line of pressure ridges, tumbled blocks and jagged plates of ice thrust up like miniature, illogical mountains a quarter mile from shore. Svarten picked an easy passage through the obstacles, and with Ivar lifting and shoving on the back of the sled, they soon reached less jumbled sea ice.

For a week now, in the full and growing light, he and the huskies had been on the go, prowling Hornsund from Bird Mountain to Halfway Bowl. The traplines were shut down, for soon the foxes would begin seeking mates. From now until the snow and ice disappeared in the first warm winds of May or June or July, he would be constantly on the move, driving himself to exhaustion and his team to footsore, rib-showing thinness, racing up and down the fjord in search of the white bears.

But even in this frenetic season he stopped to savor the piercing turquoise of glacier fronts and the clear silver flow of sunlight down rugged mountainsides, and for a moment he knew a desire to share the wild beauty of the land. Then the team whimpered impatiently and he was racing off again, looking for creamy shadows moving over the radiant, blue-white ice.

The four bears he had taken in the dark were nearly half

Out on the sea ice

of his quota. While he was not unhappy with any of the pelts, he wanted to make sure that his six remaining bears were prime males. Ten bears. Far less than his first year, when he and Fredrik had taken more than fifty. It had been an exciting time for Ivar; he had come to the Arctic for adventure, and he had found it in hunting polar bears.

But as Ivar's first year as a hunter blended with his second and third years, he changed. Hunting became a job; killing was neither enjoyed nor despised. He learned that if you would live like the polar bear, you must kill with as little feeling, as little pleasure or remorse, as the bears did. By his fourth year his satisfaction came from being a part of the Arctic, alone and free.

If Ivar had been wealthy enough to live in Hornsund without hunting, he would have done so gladly. But few people have enough money to live without working. In order to pay for his fourth year in the Arctic, Ivar needed each of the ten bears the government allowed him to take, plus all the foxes he could trap. Next year he would also be allowed ten bears. The year after—none. No bears, no foxes, no seals, no geese or ducks, nothing but ptarmigan.

Yet Ivar did not fight the new laws. He respected the great white bears. He had lived with them and watched them, been hunted by them and hunted them in turn. Huge and graceful, savage and patient, to Ivar the bears were the essence of the high Arctic. But he did resent being forced out of his chosen home by thoughtless summer "hunters" who searched the sea with power boats and shot the helpless bears as they swam. Too often the bear sank before it could be retrieved. And even if the dead bear was brought aboard, a summer pelt was worthless for display. The result was that summer-killed bears were traded for a winter-killed pelt.

Each summer too many bears were slaughtered and wasted.

The easiest way for the government to end the abuse was to ban all bear hunting, even by men who lived alone in the Arctic and met the polar bear on its own terms.

'But the ban was not enough. Polar bears were not safe just because they were no longer hunted. The wandering bears needed the whole Arctic, wide and free and wild. An environment nibbled to death by heavy commercial sealing and over-fishing and oil drilling and mining was as dangerous to the bears' survival as unbridled hunting—and more cruel. A bullet was kinder than starvation.

Ivar rested the team for a moment and stood in the middle of the light-filled land. Wind blew curls of dry snow across the ice beyond the pressure ridges. He struck out toward the center of the fjord, looking for bear sign on the hard-packed surface of the sea ice. He had yet to see a bear this week, although he had seen plenty of tracks across the snow. Most of the tracks led eastward, down Hornsund toward the closed end of the fjord, across the island to the eastern coast of Spitsbergen.

He had discussed the bears' pattern of movement with scientists from the Polar Institute and with every old hunter he had ever met. The answer was always the same. Polar bears moved in a giant circle around Spitsbergen, coming down out of the northwest with the pack ice in spring, crossing or circling to the east coast, then following the ice highways and drifting pack ice north as the sun pushed back the cold. By summer the bears' wanderings had taken them to Northeast Land, the most northern of the Svalbard Islands, or onto the pack ice that circled the North Pole. In fall the bears moved south again, by land or by sea ice, following their own noses and an age-old urge out of the barren regions of winter to spots like Hornsund, where ringed seals denned up in spring to give birth. Then across the island, at Hornsund or Bellsund or Isfjorden, and the circle began again.

On hunting trips like this one, Ivar worked out onto the ice, where he was most likely to find fresh bear sign. Most of the time polar bears kept to the ice or the shoreline, wherever travel was easiest. He preferred hunting on sea ice, for it gave him a better chance to spot the bears and to gauge their size from far away. He wanted every chance to avoid a confrontation with a bear that was not a prime male. The intense spring sunlight had allowed him to remount on the Mauser the telescopic sight, which doubled as a spyglass. Open sights were mandatory at night, but night was over. Now he wanted every advantage he could get, both for himself and for the bear.

A mile offshore he spotted the faint indented trail of a bear on the move. The dogs scented bear. Svarten veered to intersect the tracks, stopping to put his nose into the pad depressions where the edges were serrated by claw gouges. As he caught the fullness of the bear's scent from the tracks, Svarten huffed softly. The fur on his ruff lifted and he raised his long black muzzle into the wind. The team moved restlessly in their harness.

Ivar quieted the huskies and knelt by the trail. The wind made judgments tricky, but the fine dusting of snow in the depressions indicated that the tracks were at most a few hours old. He straightened and lifted the rifle to his shoulder, scanning the horizon through the scope. No movement to the east, the direction in which the tracks led.

He knelt again and measured the tracks with his hands; nearly twice as long as his fingers and palm, and as wide as his hand placed sideways. A rather large bear, and alone. Probably a male on the prowl, or perhaps a very old female.

He scanned the horizon again. Nothing moved but windblown snow. He turned the team east and followed the bear's trail. The first bears of the spring migration were often fat and healthy, moving fast and easily across the roughest terrain.

As he had expected, the trail veered toward a shallow bay. He lost the tracks in a tumbled pile of glacier and sea ice. For a few minutes he cast around the edges of the pileup, but the iron-hard snow yielded no more tracks. If the bear kept on its former heading, it would end up in the mountains east of Main Cabin. The passes there were few and hair-raising, as he knew only too well.

Curious, he headed the team east, following the tracks. The huskies trotted easily, the sound of their passage drowned by the humming, moaning wind. Beneath the wind he became aware of a strange, very faint noise. He strained toward it, hardly believing his ears. A bear. Angry and rumbling and very far away, muffled by the wind.

He stopped the team and listened carefully. The sounds came again, clearer but still faint, from somewhere on shore. He searched the rocks and flatlands for some sign of the bear. Nothing. Not even a track up the ice foot and onto the flatlands.

Again the sound, but so faint he could not pinpoint its source. He lifted the rifle to his shoulder and scanned the shore-line, where storm surf and tidal surges had sculpted fantastic ice shapes. Nothing. But he was not imagining things—Svarten had heard the bear, too. The husky's head was up, ears cocked to catch the sounds. Ivar held his breath and listened. And still he could not locate the origin of the low complaints.

He lowered the rifle and turned away from the shore for a moment. Sometimes the wind and rocky cliffs played games with sound, gathering a noise from behind and bouncing it back on itself. But there were no bears behind him. Nothing but ice.

Bear tracks

He turned back toward the shore and slowly swept the ice foot with the scope, studying the flatlands behind. Nothing. He raised his eyes again, examining the base of the rugged mountain slopes. The wind paused for a moment and the sound came clearly. Higher, way up the mountain. There, tiny in the distance, a creamy blur on the blue-white snow. The bear was more than halfway up a steep, bowl-like depression in the mountainside, climbing, heading for a notch between two peaks and growling to itself at the difficulty of the path it had chosen.

The rifle scope brought the bear close enough to show the shuffling gait, the head down and swaying side to side as the bear walked across the hard-packed snow of the little bowl. A male, and a handsome beast, large even at this distance. His coat was so full it looked fluffy, altogether at odds with the tireless power of his shambling walk.

Ivar watched the bear for several minutes, laughing silently at the rumbling complaints that rose and fell in counterpoint to the wind. The bear went where he wished to go, then complained as he went, never quite sure why he had not chosen an easier trail. That was a bear Ivar could understand. The bear could have been only 80 yards away and his finger would have stayed off the trigger; there was something funny and fine about the solitary, muttering animal. He watched until the bear clawed his way to the top of the bowl and disappeared through the notch.

Good hunting, my friend. And smoother passes!

Still chuckling, he lowered his rifle and turned the team back onto the sea ice. As they worked their way northeast, toward Hans Glacier's vivid turquoise face, the wind blew hard and steady, making razor-edged drift snow race in knee-high billows. The dogs trotted, heads down against the wind, across the bay in front of Hans Glacier. The air was so cold and dry

*Ivar and Naika. Ice humps in
background are freshwater (glacier)
ice frozen into sea ice*

that it felt brittle. Though the sun was high, it could not yet warm the polar air masses that flowed down over Hornsund.

Like the dogs, Ivar moved with his head slightly down, looking up only to check that he was not getting too close to the glacier's icy terminus. For all the intense cold, glaciers occasionally calved in winter and spring. Not often, but he would not get much closer to the glacier without a very good reason. At this point, even a prime bear pelt was not a good enough reason.

He had plenty of time to take bears, more than sixty days of the maddeningly beautiful spring, white and blue and glittering with light. It was the best time of the year. The mountains were carved out of crystal; every shadow had a lambent blue life of its own, and the horizon was a diamond line of ice punctuated by pale, blue-green glacier fronts. As he looked around, he felt a small ache inside his mind, a nameless, subtle sadness.

All winter you complain of the darkness, and when the light finally comes you're still not happy. What more do you want? What could be better than this?

You're changing. Last year it was enough to be young and alive and living in Hornsund.

The interior changing he felt was elusive. He left it where he had found it. He would live with it until he understood, then he would act.

Further up the fjord, he veered away from the land, toward long, ragged pressure ridges in the fjord ice. Seals sometimes gathered around the fractured ice, and where there were seals there might be bears.

As the wind whistled in from the fractured ice, he stopped the dogs and unslung his rifle to scan the pressure ridges. Three quarters of a mile away, partially hidden by an upthrust chunk of ice, he saw the dark oval shape of a ringed seal. The supply of seal meat at Main Cabin was a little low; soon the dogs should have bear to eat, but it would be foolish to pass up seal today in hope of bear tomorrow.

He began to maneuver into position. He found a spot where tidal pressure had thrown up a broad plate of ice and moved the team behind it. With the dogs tethered to a piece of ice and Naika tethered to the sled, he was free to begin a careful stalk.

He circled around pressure ridges, always keeping at least one ragged ice barrier between himself and the sunning seal. As he stalked, the wind faded to an occasional icy sigh. He removed his skis and eased forward on foot.

After ten minutes, he calculated that he was less than 100 yards away from the seal. Cautiously, slowly, he crept up to the last, waist-high pressure ridge and peered over. The seal was gone; all that marked its passing was a small dark hole through shining ice.

He swore silently, wondering how he had given himself away. Of course, the seal might simply have gotten hungry and returned to the black water to fish. Perhaps it would surface again nearby, at another in the series of breathing holes that each seal maintained.

He scanned the ice through his rifle scope, but saw no fat dark forms on the ice. Then a vague suggestion of motion caught his eye 300 yards upwind, behind another, higher pressure ridge. Though he had seen nothing more than a subtle shift in color, a faint off-white against the blue-white of snow, he knew it had to be a bear.

Even before the thought registered consciously, he was crouched down and trotting toward the seal's breathing hole. The bear might have been stalking the seal, too. Though the seal had vanished beneath the ice, there was a good chance that the bear would move in to wait in ambush beside the hole. Two could play that game.

By the time Ivar flopped beside the breathing hole, the bear was still more than 200 yards off. Quietly, he unslung his rifle and waited.

But when he spotted the bear again, it was heading away. Nothing in its movements suggested hurry or fright; it was simply snuffling among the pressure ridges, hoping to smell its next meal. He watched the bear long enough to assure himself that it was male, above average size and beautifully furred. The wind held low and steady, blowing from the bear to him. He lay without moving, hoping that the bear would glance over and spot the dark, seal-like blot against the snow, an opportunity that no bear would pass up.

The bear continued on his course, out and away from Ivar. Ivar hesitated, then whistled through his teeth, a shrill rising sound that carried far over the ice. Through the scope he saw the bear's head turn. Ivar swung his feet up and down, imitating the motion of a seal's rear flippers. In an instant the bear shifted into hunting movements, low and sinuous and swift. With the controlled grace that always amazed Ivar, the white bear flowed behind a small pressure ridge and vanished.

He waited, knowing the bear would reappear. But where? Left? Right? He raised his eyes above the scope and waited. Though he doubted that the bear would come straight out of the wind, he checked the area ahead anyway.

The bear materialized on the left, 100 yards away. There were no more pressure ridges, only random chunks and hummocks of ice. The bear would move more slowly now, stalking the dark seal-shape with the immense patience unique to predators.

Testing the wind

With equal patience Ivar watched the stalk, admiring the consummate skill that allowed the bear to melt behind small ice humps and flow over open spaces. When there was nothing but flat ice left, the bear stretched low, slithering forward, a gliding white silence 50 yards away.

Ivar waited and watched. He could see the long, thick fur feathers behind the front legs fan out as the bear moved forward. Occasionally he caught a vague whispering sigh, but if he had not known the bear was near, he would have assumed it was just the sound of windblown snow crystals.

Slowly, one muscle at a time, Ivar eased into firing position. His subtle movements froze the bear in place. Ivar could see the black shine of the eyes, but the black nose was lost behind a reaching paw.

The two hunters waited, motionless.

After a full minute the bear resumed his gliding stalk. Ivar waited and felt tension building. As long as the bear approached head on and flattened to the ice, Ivar's only target was the broad white forehead. He preferred a spine or heart shot. He could be sure of only one bullet; it had better be all he needed.

The polar bear was less than 30 yards away. A running bear could cover 30 yards in seconds.

Ivar waited, breathing slowly, shallowly. The bear was oozing closer with each breath and still Ivar's only target was the thick skull that could deflect an 8mm bullet. If the bear came much closer, even a heart shot might not kill quickly enough.

A subtle ripple of muscles beneath thick white fur signaled the potent ingathering of a bear about to charge. Ivar shifted the rifle barrel slightly to compensate for the scope setting of 100 yards. If he had had time, he could have counted each hair on the bear's forehead, but the ice seemed to explode as the bear surged forward.

Twenty-five yards—wait, not yet. Twenty—still only the

forehead. Eighteen-sixteen-twelve-ten—skull swinging aside. Now!

As the rifle bucked against his shoulder, the bear slid in eerie slow motion that stopped only 20 feet away. The metallic click of the rifle bolt seemed as loud as the shot had been, louder than the echo rolling back from the mountains. But nothing was as loud as the enraged roar dying in the white bear's throat.

Ivar lifted his head from the scope, and his breath rushed out in a long sigh. Too close. Without taking eyes or rifle off the inert bear, he pulled himself slowly upright. Standing, he could see a small scarlet circle spreading slowly, high up on the neck. He started to move closer, but his legs responded sluggishly; unlike a seal, he was not equipped to lie motionless on ice. He stumbled slightly and looked down for better footing. Almost instantly, he returned his attention to the bear.

The back eyes were open. He could not remember if that was a change. Without getting closer he inspected the bear again. His hunter's sixth sense was alert, though he knew that no animal could survive a spine shot from 20 feet.

No flickering eyelids, no twitch of muscle, nothing. Yet the stain of blood on the neck seemed larger. Some residual life must remain, pumping bright blood over white fur, heart beating, blood flowing, time slowing. With dreamlike disinterest, Ivar watched as the bear surged upright, front claws gouging, diamond ice chips flying and the world a long, deep growl. Reflex, not thought, brought the rifle up and triggered a second shot into the bear's heaving shoulder, but reflex would have been too slow had not the hindquarters given way, transforming a fluid lunge into a futile slide.

Even as he leaped backward, Ivar tripped a third shell into the chamber. The bear was quiet again—and less than 10 feet away. With the rifle trained on the near shoulder, Ivar circled around the white form, waiting for any further sign of life. He came up from the rear, reached out with rifle barrel and prodded the flank. No twitch. Rifle barrel on the head, he moved forward again, watched the vacant, half-closed eye. No flicker of reflex, even when cold metal touched naked eye. The bear was finally dead.

With his eyes, Ivar measured the bear. He was a big animal, more than 9 feet from nose to tail. The pelt was superb, heavy and white, and the long fur behind the front legs lifted gently in the wind. The best bear of the year.

Crouching, Ivar inspected the two wounds. He was disappointed that he had needed two shots—and disturbed that he had taken so long to get off the second one. The first shot had been a fraction too high. It had missed severing the spinal cord, but the shock wave of the bullet's passage must have damaged the nerves controlling the rear legs. Were it not for that, the bear would have finished his leap and killed him as easily as a careless seal. Just a quarter inch either way would have meant the bear's instant death at the first shot or Ivar's before the second. Ivar had been lucky.

He propped the rifle against the body and knelt to examine the broad skull. There was a lopsidedness about the face that intrigued him. When he rolled the heavy head onto the right side, he found that the left cheek was virtually gone, smashed in by an accident that not even time and scar tissue and thick fur could conceal.

As he parted the fur, he was appalled to find that the skull felt mushy. Only the skin protected the brain. It was a ghastly wound; even now, years later, it was an agony to see.

On a sudden suspicion, he peeled off his gloves and kneaded his fingers through the fur below the wound. His fingertips found and traced long, parallel scar ridges. . . the wound was the result of a fight with another bear. Obviously this bear had survived a direct blow, the kind that jellied a seal's brains. The bear's skull had been laid open to the soft brain, but the bear had survived. And not only survived, but moved and hunted with liquid grace. No wonder this bear had survived Ivar's first shot; he was far too tough to be killed by a near miss.

For a long moment Ivar stared at the crushed head, weighing and appreciating the mystery of the bear's immense determination to live. But then his hands ached with cold, and he was reminded of his own imperatives. He picked up his rifle and went back to retrieve his skis and the impatient dogs.

Svarten was the first to catch bear scent on his hands. The husky's black ruff flared until Ivar quieted him with reassuring words. He moved the team closer to the seal's breathing hole and waited until the dogs accepted the idea that the bear was dead. When the team quieted, he untied Naika; she knew enough to stay out of his way while he worked.

He settled down to the careful, strenuous, bloody work of skinning out a polar bear. When he was finished, he loaded a quarter ton of meat, plus the heavy pelt, onto the sled. The dogs would earn their dinner today. Just as he finished tying the pelt on top of the rapidly freezing meat, he heard a faint sound, high and wild above the wind.

He scanned the ice first, immediately suspecting more bears. Nothing moved on the horizon. Then the sound came again, and with it recognition. He raised the rifle and scanned the west until he saw two dots closing in. Ivory gulls, pale against the sky.

The birds dropped lower, silent now. Their round black eyes stared at him over short black beaks and their bodies curved pure white above ebony feet. Somehow the gulls had known that flesh was here to be eaten. In time the first foxes would appear, drawn as mysteriously as the birds.

While he checked the load on the sled, the ivory gulls

Glaucous gull on bear carcass

circled above him like tiny white angels of death, crying their hunger in piercing tones.

He led the team 50 feet away and turned back to watch. The gulls hesitated, then swooped down and began to feed. Within moments the elegant white scavengers were slurred with blood.

The white bear dies and the white birds feed. Foxes and huskies and even other bears will also eat. When the melt comes, whatever remains will sink into the fjord, feeding krill that feed fish that feed seals that feed bears. The Arctic uses every scrap of life again and again. If it had been my flesh, it would be no different.

We all feast on strength and life, every living creature in the world. I don't know why people shrink from the deaths that make their lives possible.

He turned the huskies back toward Main Cabin. The spring sun was still above the western horizon, cold and bronze, as he climbed through the small slot in the ice foot and up the shore to the cabin.

In the second week of April, a harsh wind swept in from the sea, blurring the sun with clouds and flying snow. Ivar was caught in Main Cabin, but spring winds lacked the claustrophobic impact of winter storms. This time he actually enjoyed being cabinbound, resting and eating. Especially eating. The last month of constant travel had drawn his skin taut over muscle and bone; he had lost every particle of fat. While the storm lasted, he would eat five meals a day.

Usually he ate only twice a day during the spring, morning and night, each meal providing perhaps two thousand calories. It was not enough. During the endless morning light, when he traveled eighteen hours a day, he always went from

Storm coming over Arctic Ocean

lean to thin to skinny. Like the dogs and the bears, he lost his winter reserves of blubber in the icy sunlit spring. He also lost water to the dry air. He drank more liquids than seemed reasonable, or even possible. His eyes saw only frozen water, and no thirst, but his body was not fooled; at 30 below zero, there was no free water in the air. A Hornsund spring desiccated as efficiently as a Sahara summer.

When he could hold no more food or drink or sleep, the storm provided entertainment. In the eerie, sourceless storm light, racing clouds and snow created shifting arctic Rorschachs that were by turns wild and savage, dreamy and serene.

Four springs ago, during the short period Fredrik and Ivar had shared Main Cabin, Fredrik sat at this window watching a similar storm while Ivar played the crazy fool—at least, that was one of the things Fredrik called him. Ivar had been restless, as usual, and had gone to Cabin Bay. When he was ready to go back to Main Cabin, the weather was bad, but not ugly enough to keep him at Cabin Bay. With the wind at his back, he could make good time skiing.

He got all the way to Fox Valley before the wind became more hurricane than gale. He could barely stay upright. He soon realized that he was not skiing the storm, the storm was skiing him. He blew before the wind like an awkward, rectangular sail. At some point he lost his ski poles, but kept his balance by spreading his arms like a high-wire walker.

He had never skied faster, not even behind a runaway team on a downhill glacier. He was flying, wild and free as the gyrfalcon, soaring on the storm. He should have been frightened but he was having too much fun.

He fell once or twice, but always managed to get his skis under him again before he rolled out of control. It was not until he came whizzing up to Main Cabin that he realized he was going to have a tricky time getting off the merry-go-round. The wind was a lot stronger than he was. Even if he threw himself flat on the ground, he would not stop until he smashed into something heavier than he was.

He hit a small rise just west of the cabin and was airborne before he knew it. He went end over end past the cabin without touching the ground. Hanging upside down, he caught a glimpse of Fredrik's surprised face through the cabin window.

Fredrik was up from the table and out the door before Ivar made a crash landing against a pile of boulders downwind from the cabin, where he lay against the rocks catching his breath and checking that he had the proper number of arms and legs.

Though on foot, Fredrik was little better off with the wind. He had to crawl toward Ivar by pulling himself along on whatever was within reach. That the mishap was not Ivar's fault, he was sure Fredrik would understand. They might even have a good laugh about it, especially the moment when Ivar sailed past the cabin window.

Fredrik was not amused. Two days later, when he began speaking to Ivar again, he told Ivar exactly what kind of a fool he was for ever leaving Cabin Bay.

The storm ended three days later. It had lasted just long enough to make Ivar eager to be out again. He fed the dogs from the carcass of the seventh bear, killed two days before the storm on the ice in front of Main Cabin, and set off to explore the storm-changed land.

On the fjord ice, new-blown snow lay 4 or 5 inches deep, dry and powdery. Behind him stretched parallel ski tracks, pale-blue shadow lines across the shimmering snow. Ahead were ice and mountains and an endless fall of light, a reborn world in which anything seemed possible.

He skied easily, enjoying the exercise after forced idleness. His eyes roamed the ice, looking for anything unusual. After less than a mile, he saw in the distance a broad, meandering trail. At first he thought it might have been made by a bearded seal, trapped by closing ice and hauling its massive body across the frozen fjord, seeking a way beneath the lid of ice.

But as he skied up to the trail, he saw long claw gouges that could only have been made by a bear. A soundless whistle escaped his lips as he measured the tracks with his eyes.

Hello, grandfather. My God, but you're huge!

He knelt beside the tracks, still only half believing. Each paw mark was the shape and size of a small washtub. Sometime after the wind had dropped, the bear had shuffled through the new snow, heading east.

He unslung the rifle and scanned the trail across the ice; the tracks marked the snow to the limit of the scope, but there was no giant bear in sight. He reslung the rifle and skied along the trail. From time to time he glanced down at the tracks, still not quite able to believe his eyes.

He skied for hours in the cold light, thoroughly warming his body, yet careful not to raise sweat that would turn to ice the second he.stopped moving. The incredible wallowing trail unreeled ahead of him into the distance, no fresher than when he had found it. The sameness of skiing across the snow-layered ice was broken only by the small progress he measured against the mountains along the fjord. He was past Missing Mountain now, and Bird Mountain's massif had grown significantly.

He stopped for ten minutes, melting snow for water, and then pushed on. He would quite willingly ski the length of the fjord—twice—just to see the bear that made those gigantic tracks.

Another hour of travel brought him opposite the spot where one of his inland trails to Bird Mountain came down through a narrow slot and onto the ice. Familiar ground, and very rough. When the tracks veered in toward land, he stopped to melt more drinking water. The bear was heading for an area of tumbled rocks and uneven terrain where snow drifted deeply. It was an ideal place for a bear to den up and a dangerous place to hunt. It would be too easy to become hunted rather than hunter.

But those tracks. The biggest bear he had ever killed had been just over 10 feet long and had left tracks much smaller than these. The least he could do was follow the trail a little further before he decided it was too dangerous to go on.

The huge tracks went ashore, right into the deepest drifts and biggest boulders. He stopped 50 yards out on the ice and scanned the area through the rifle scope. The tracks moved up over the ice foot and disappeared inland. He considered skirting the rocky area and coming ashore further east, then doubling back, hoping to pick up the trail on better ground. But there was no guarantee that the bear had turned east. If he took the time to climb the slope, the bear might go northeast, out of sight among the rugged interior mountains.

Ivar took off his skis, jammed them upright in the snow next to the poles, and prepared to follow the tantalizing tracks. With the heavy Mauser beneath his right arm, he scrambled up the 3-foot shore break and moved slowly along the trail, his eyes warily checking the land ahead. For fifteen minutes he followed the giant prints, listening, listening for any sound beyond snow crystals rubbing over each other in the wind. In sheltered depressions and the lee of rockpiles, snow puffed out from his boots like deep breaths. Farther inland not even the wind was alive; the only sound was the shore ice settling on the outgoing tide.

Yet some inner sense insisted that the bear was nearby.

He did not question the knowledge; he used it gratefully. When he came to a passage between two head-high boulders, he listened for a long moment, then left the trail to circle above the uphill boulder.

From a vantage point above the boulder, he saw that the trail curved around a deep drift in the lee of the hill, then vanished. He glanced around quickly, trying to locate the bear. An animal that size did not just disappear. It had to be somewhere nearby. Motionless, he listened. His heart quickened as he heard the muffled sound of a bear's breathing, followed by the soft, scraping noise of snow being rearranged by paws rather than wind. The sounds came from around the curve of the hill, near the point where the trail disappeared. Yet he still could see neither the bear nor the place where it might have entered the drift.

Cautiously, he went farther upslope and was rewarded by a view of the tracks doubling back into the drift. He could even see a round blue shadow, the hole where the bear had burrowed into the drift to build a snow cave. It must still be inside, perhaps getting ready to sleep off a huge meal.

He drew a slow breath, held it, exhaled. A quick survey of the surrounding terrain convinced him that he already was in the best position to take on a giant bear; upslope advantage, loaded rifle, finger on trigger. When the blue entry hole filled the rifle sight, he shouted as loudly as he could.

The sound seemed as large as an avalanche to him, but the only response it drew was a muffled grumble from inside the drift. No movement. The King was not about to be disturbed.

He yelled again, loud enough to bring an echo rolling back down the slope. Not even a grumble this time. He shouted again and again in spite of the frigid air burning his throat and lungs with each deep breath.

No movement whatsoever. This polar bear was big enough to fear nothing and full enough not to be curious about a potential meal shouting on his doorstep.

Ivar lowered the rifle but kept an eye on the cave entrance 50 feet away. With the rifle resting inside his arm, he scooped three fist-sized chunks of crusted snow. He pitched one toward the den, lifting the rifle to his shoulder before the fragment disappeared into the drift. He expected an angry bear to come charging out, but nothing happened. No further sound or movement. He swore in exasperation and threw the second chunk of snow. His aim was excellent; a shower of snow fell through the opening. No response.

Goddamned lazy bear. I ought to slide down and kick him right in his lazy ass.

A glance at the size of the paw prints squelched that impulse. He raised the rifle and sent a round through the top of the drift. Snow fountained as the bear came straight through the side of the drift; he looked like a white whale but moved like a cat.

In one motion Ivar snapped a second shell into the chamber, aimed and fired. The bullet caught the charging bear in the chest, slowing him long enough for Ivar to ram a new cartridge home. He squeezed the trigger and heard the thud of the second bullet striking flesh before the echo of the first shot rolled back down the slope. The bear staggered to one side, wavered on his feet, then rolled backward into the snowdrift.

Ivar waited and watched the half-buried form. Both bullets had gone into the chest, and he did not trust chest shots. When there was no further movement from below, he let out his breath and lowered the rifle. He felt his way down the slope slowly, never taking his eyes off the broad back and rump, which were all he could see of the bear. No rise and fall of white flank, no sign of life. Unless he wanted to dig out the head, he had no way of being certain the bear was dead. If the bear were not dead, he had no business digging close to those long white teeth.

He prodded the bulging hindquarters with his boot. When there was no movement, he drew back his foot and gave the bear a resounding kick. Not so much as a muscle twitched. He circled cautiously to the side, getting a better view of the flank. He waited a moment, then decided the bear was as dead as any he had ever seen. With the downhill slope, a shove on the shoulder should get the carcass rolled onto its back, ready for skinning. He reached out to shove the bear, then hesitated.

Don't be stupid—a rifle bullet only costs a dime.

He pushed the rifle barrel down and under the bear's left shoulder until the muzzle was pressed firmly into the flesh. At this range and angle, there was no way he could miss the heart. Fully expecting nothing to happen, he squeezed the trigger.

The bear rose in an explosion of snow and rage. The first shots had only stunned him, but even his huge strength could not transcend the last bullet deep in his heart. The huge white body slipped over onto its back, slid partway downhill and was still again.

Ivar jumped backward, working another shell into the chamber. He knew the bear could not survive a heart shot, but he waited just the same. When his own heartbeat returned to normal, he walked slowly toward the massive white head. There was no flicker of response when he raked the barrel across the eye.

He stepped away, rolled a cigarette and studied the dead bear. He was large, but not as large as Ivar had expected. A big male, to be sure, as big as any he had shot, but not a monster. Where had the tracks come from? Mystified, he checked the bear's hind feet—and laughed aloud. The long feathers of fur around the paws were matted and stiff with ice, nearly doubling the size of the paws, as though the bear had worn snowshoes. But . . . only sick or injured bears neglected their fur like that, and nothing about this bear's movements had suggested a lack of health.

He smoked his cigarette, puzzling over this second mystery. By all appearances the bear was fit. His coat was full and thick and white, his sides and flanks utterly round with blubber. In fact, the bear was about half again as wide as any bear he had ever seen. Positively obese.

Ivar laughed again, softly, as he realized he had found the answer. The bear had been so fat that he could not even turn around to clean the ice off his heels.

With the last of his cigarette finished, Ivar pulled his skinning knife and went to work. The pelt was flawless, full and smooth as thick silk threads. No scars, new or old. Even the muzzle was white with fur. Though the bear had not lived up to his footprints, getting him was well worth the effort. Ivar had never felt a finer pelt. This one would be his. No broker or rug maker or taxidermist would buy this skin for money. This one belonged to Ivar Ruud.

Working swiftly, deftly, he skinned the bear, then folded and buried the pelt. As soon as he got back to the cabin, he would bring the dogs up here to haul the beautiful fur to safety.

The days of April were running away from him. More than three weeks were gone already. His work was largely finished; all but the frozen bears had been scraped, and the pelts were curing in salt. He had taken nine bears and passed up many times that number. He was a little worried about taking the tenth bear; he could not count on time and ice enough for more than one last hunt.

Eighteen foxes, half a year's work

The morning light never left Hornsund now. The sun made a daily, sweeping elipse above the mountains, pouring white light over the icy fjord. Where rock pockets caught the sun and reflected it, the temperature nudged within a few degrees of thawing. As he looked at the glistening land around Main Cabin, he sensed that the flawless crystal spring would all too soon melt into summer.

The realization brought sadness. He loved this time of year better than any other—the quality of the light, the pristine snow, the magnificent austerity of ice and sky and polished mountain peaks. Life went into the Arctic's primal crucible and came out changed, refined, melded into a seamless whole, and spring was the time of realization.

Spring was a gyrfalcon, alive in white flight.

A new, bittersweet dimension came to his appreciation of the moment. The wild, headstrong kid who had come here four years ago had become a hard-muscled, self-controlled man. Hornsund had forged him. But while he changed, the world also changed. People in crowded cities built a barrier of rules around the Arctic.

He sat motionlessly beside the cabin window, ice-blue eyes brooding over the shining land. Then his chair grated in the quiet room as he rose and pulled on a jacket. He had promised himself a fresh ptarmigan dinner; staring out the window would not get it.

Naika stood eagerly by the door, her eyes bright with hope. He let her out, gathered the heavy Mauser and the light .22 and walked out into the sun-filled world. As he circled around to the back of the cabin, he told Naika to stay behind with the huskies. Her tail drooped, then lifted again as she trotted over to Svarten. Any other dog would have been greeted with a wicked flash of teeth, but Naika was a female. As far as the all-male team was concerned, Naika walked on water.

Ptarmigan trails on feeding ground

Ivar skied over the crusty snow behind Main Cabin, heading for Ptarmigan Slope. In late spring and summer, sea birds swarmed over the talus slope, building or burrowing nests to raise their young. The breeding multitudes drove the ptarmigan inland, but left a thin layer of droppings that fed the grass. When the transient birds left, the ptarmigan returned to bulge their crops with nourishing seeds.

Today the ptarmigan should be out, poking through the crusted snow, gathering last summer's seeds before the noisy sea birds returned. It would not be too long now; already he had seen a few pale-gray glaucous gulls scavenging over the sea ice. Even the surface of the snow was subtly changing. Tiny opaque flakes were being transformed by sun warmth into slightly larger, transparent granules.

He took off his skis and picked a diagonal trail up the slope, working toward the chute he had fallen down four years before. He stopped long enough to open his jacket; climbing with his back to the wind had made him rather warm. As he rested he looked around for ptarmigan. He had heard a few of the chuckling, clucking sounds characteristic of feeding ptarmigan, but he had not spotted the birds yet. They were somewhere nearby. Finally he spotted a ptarmigan only 20 feet away. The bird was resting in a tiny hollow, blending almost perfectly into the surrounding snow. Had it not been for the bird's black-button eyes, he would have missed it completely.

Slowly he raised the .22 and aimed at the liquid curve of neck, where pure white feathers glowed like pearls. The jet black eyes watched without fear, and the flawless satin body remained utterly still. With a sigh he lowered the gun. He was not hungry enough to shoot that particular ptarmigan. There would be other, less perfect birds further up the slope. He tucked the .22 under his arm and resumed climbing.

Before he reached the top of the slope, several dinners

Male ptarmigan in winter colors

were assured; five fat ptarmigan rested in his rucksack. There were many more of the round white birds in sight, moving on feathered feet among the rocks and ice, but he did not shoot them. He had what he needed; now he could relax and enjoy the chuckling, feeding ptarmigan that looked more like animated snowballs than proper birds.

He searched along the ridge top until he found a rock that was flat and free of ice. The cold wind sighed up the slope, blowing just hard enough to make him glad to button his jacket again. He rolled a cigarette and surveyed the land beneath him.

The fjord was still a silver swath of ice except toward the middle, where tidal surges had forced small leads through it, spilling frigid salt water onto the snow. The narrow, blue-black fingers were harbingers of the breakup. Five weeks, maybe a little bit more, and the governor's trim ship would enter Hornsund. Before that, not more than two weeks from today, the birds would return. Geese and ducks, guillemots and dovekies and all the other birds would take up their breeding stations on reefs and cliffs and rocks and flatlands, and Hornsund would ring with the million voices of summer.

The tortured groans of sea ice rose up the slope. The tide was turning, water flowing out from beneath broad plates of ice, narrow leads closing, ice grinding as it adjusted to the changing sea. To the west, beyond the mouth of the fjord, he could just make out a low black cloud of moisture condensed over open water; the Arctic Ocean was splitting out of its ice cocoon. Soon, too soon, Hornsund would be a deep blue surge of water caught between bare stone mountains.

He looked away from the sea, down to where Main Cabin was a rectangular box no bigger than his hand. The dogs were tiny black dots against the snow. In front of the cabin, a billion snow crystals transformed yellow sunlight into every shade of blue. And out from the cabin, a pale suggestion of movement.

He unslung his Mauser and scanned the ice through the scope. It took several sweeping arcs before he found the bear— or bears, this time. A mother and two cubs. She moved up the fjord at a steady swinging pace, the gait of a bear that has a particular destination in mind. The silver-white cubs were barely a sixth of their mother's size. They tumbled over each other and her and their own feet with the heedless energy of youth.

He sat for long minutes, savoring the rare chance to watch cubs in safety. Mother bears guarded their young with awesome savagery, for male bears had no compunctions about killing cubs. Once, the female stopped and cuffed the cubs into silence. Then she stood, long neck weaving back and forth as she tested the wind. She must have scented the dogs and decided to avoid a possible source of danger. She veered further out onto the fjord, leading her cubs in a wide arc around the cabin. They all disappeared behind a pressure ridge. As he put the rifle aside, he became aware of the numbing cold seeping into his body from the slope. Summer might be coming, but it was not here yet. Time to get moving.

An hour later, Ivar was almost at the bottom of the slope when the wind carried up the sounds of an aroused pack of huskies. He could not see the dogs, but he did not have to see in order to know what was happening. That crescendo of rage could only mean a bear was very close to them.

He went down the last part of the slope in a leaping, sliding run. Usually bears avoided the dogs, or at most sniffed around a bit and then wandered off. Though chained, the huskies made formidable opponents. But that was no reason to dawdle. If this was one of the rare bears that was determined to have a dog dinner, he should be there to help the team. And Naika.

He strapped on his skis and covered the distance to Main Cabin in record time. When he came around the corner of the cabin, rifle ready, he saw the huskies straining at the ends of their long chains, silent except for an occasional deep snarl. And Naika stood among them, fur erect and long teeth bared, wild as a wolf.

The bear was nowhere to be seen. Only tracks remained, making a wide, ragged circle around the huskies.

He praised and quieted the dogs as he followed the tracks around them. Obviously the bear had looked the dogs over, decided they were more fight than food and left. But it could not be far off, and its tracks were large enough to make his blood quicken.

He skied alongside the crisp tracks. Naika moved after him, still wild. The trail went over the ice foot and out onto the fjord. He scanned the ice until he spotted the white bear going away, heading out toward distant ranks of pressure ridges where less fierce meals lay sunning on the ice. It was too late in the season to pass up a prime male. The range was extreme, even for the long-barreled Mauser, but it was the best shot he would get.

He knelt, steadied the rifle and gently squeezed off a shot. The bear seemed to stumble, then broke into a gallop, apparently unhurt. A second and third shot only kicked up chips of ice behind the bear, urging him to a faster speed. Ivar thought he had missed all three shots until he saw through the scope a red sheen of blood on the ice. The bear was wounded, though he seemed to run with undiminished strength.

Ivar turned and skied back toward the cabin. He tossed the rucksack full of ptarmigan into the storeroom, traded jacket

for heavy parka, slammed the .22 into its rack, then grabbed
Naika and chained her next to Svarten. With the Mauser slung
across his back, he skied off in pursuit of the wounded bear.

The swish of his skis was punctuated by the rhythmic
thunk of ski poles digging in for purchase and speed. The bear's
tracks made a long, shallow, west-southwest curve, heading
out to the center of the fjord.

Bright patches of red appeared along the trail. He was
surprised by the amount of bloody snow. At this rate the bear
would be dead by the time he reached the first line of pressure
ridges. But as Ivar continued skiing along the trail, he saw
that the space between the large prints did not diminish; the
bear continued to travel at a long gallop in spite of the quantities of blood left along the trail.

He skied hard, following the wounded bear. After half an
hour he noticed that the blood spoor was smaller. He was not
too surprised. He had followed other blood trails before and
had found that after a few miles the blood disappeared. Polar
bears seemed to be able to shut off the flow of blood from
wounds.

Ivar's eyes checked the ice ceaselessly, hoping to catch a
glimpse of the bear. There was nothing ahead but that first
pressure ridge, and he was far out into the fjord. He recalled
the center of the fjord as he had seen it from the top of Ptarmigan Slope, narrow black leads and blue-black shimmer of salt-
water puddles on top of unstable ice. But the ice beneath his
skis seemed secure and the wounded bear could not run for-
ever.

At the end of an hour, the blood trail shrank to an occasional thumb-sized blot on the snow, but the length of the
bear's strides seemed to have shortened. Straight ahead were
rumpled lines of pressure ridges. He leaned on his ski poles and
rested, taking quick, shallow breaths, studying the ice ahead.

Ski tracks and pressure ridge

The bear must be close to finished, if not already dead behind the pressure ridges. Where wind had scoured through snow, the ice plates under his skis showed signs of having been broken up and pushed back together recently. Yet the ice sounded and felt solid. The tracks and spots of blood were a clear trail, leading up and over a notch between two crumpled, upthrust ice plates.

He hesitated, then unslung his rifle and skied as far as he could into the jungle of jagged ice.

When his skis hampered more than they helped, he took them off and jammed them upright into a shallow snowdrift. Cautiously he pulled himself up to the top of a rough, slanting line of ice and stared ahead. The tracks continued, threading through ice obstacles. Then, 400 yards off in a flat area between two ridge lines, he saw the bear. He was moving at a fast walk, but there was a heaviness to the gait that told of weakness.

Ivar slid down the far side of the ice block and jogged along the trail, hoping to get within range, slowing only to scramble over thrusting ice. He passed the area of flat ice, but the bear was out of sight. He divided his attention between the rough ice and the possible ambush places he would have to pass, and trotted along the trail. With each exhaled breath, his beard grew thicker with ice.

Huge, crumpled plates of sea ice tilted steeply where they had ridden over each other to form yet another wide span of pressure ridges. He was nearly a mile away from his skis, deep into an area of recently fractured ice. Shadows lay everywhere, glowing blue patterns against blinding white snow. Ragged ice blocks rose above his head, burning silver in the afternoon sun. Wind moaned around him, blowing stronger than an hour ago, coming in from the Arctic Ocean, driving an increasing swell beneath the ice. Far to the northwest, storm clouds thickened the horizon.

He measured the weather signs and kept up his steady jog. The bear had to be tiring rapidly.

Another half hour of scrambling and jogging brought him to an opening, a flat snow meadow surrounded by ice peaks. Thirty feet away, the bear was stretched out on the snow. At the sound of Ivar's approach, he surged to his feet.

Ivar raised the rifle, and a single shot echoed over the ice. The bear slid back onto the snow. With cautious steps, Ivar circled the animal, watching for movement. When there was none, he nudged the nearer eye with his rifle. No response. With a last look around for other bears attractèd by fresh death, he pulled his skinning knife and knelt.

As he worked quickly, hands exposed to the deep cold, he found himself looking up more often than usual. His instincts prickled across his consciousness uneasily. By the time the bear was half skinned, the subtle warnings became urgent demands. He dropped his skinning knife next to his mittens, grabbed the Mauser and scaled the nearest block of ice to look around.

He saw a 60-foot slash of open water between himself and Hornsund's north shore, and knew a long moment when his strength drained away.

Too wide. Too cold. Is death warm?

No, LIFE is warm. Move, damn you. RUN!

Even as his mind shied away from the knowledge that he was stranded on breaking pack ice, his body was sliding down the other side of the ice block and running east, running and measuring the widening, zigzag lead. He only looked back once, and what he saw made him run faster; the lead had doubled in size. He ran on, ignoring the icy air stabbing into his lungs when shallow breaths no longer gave his body enough oxygen. He ran until the black lead narrowed to 20 feet.

Ahead the lead fanned out again.

Without stopping for thought or breath or fear, he flung his rifle across the open water. Before the rifle landed on the far side, he was swimming in the freezing sea. Three strokes took him across, booted feet kicking, bare hands reaching for purchase on the 3-foot-high ice plate. His unfeeling hands slipped, fumbled, then held long enough for a desperate pull to lift him up and out of the water.

Part of him was surprised that he felt no stunning cold. The rest of him knew nothing but a driving need to be off the breaking ice. He slung the rifle over his back and ran, beating his hands against shoulders and thighs, trying to force blood into fingers he could no longer feel. He ran and saw ice cracking off his frozen clothes, ice shifting beneath his feet, black leads opening all around him.

He ran, leaping across black water from floc to floe, balancing, running, beating white hands on icy clothes, running with a pounding heart toward a shoreline that was more than two hours away. Behind him came the wavering shrieks of ice shearing, long groans of pressure ridges falling away, endless grinding of ice disintegrating. He ran until he tripped and his palms flared into sudden pain as they broke his fall. He smiled grimly as he staggered to his feet, smiled because palms that hurt were still alive.

At some point he realized that he had cut across his own tracks and had automatically veered to follow them. He beat his hands in counterpoint to his pumping heart and ran, ran along his own tracks until legs and lungs ached, then flamed, then burned into a white eternity where thought and feeling were suspended and only his driving will was real.

He clawed up yet another pressure ridge and skidded down a ragged plate of ice. A few feet away stood his skis, dark exclamation points in the endless white. He reached, but felt nothing as his hands knocked the skis aside. He breathed on his hands and felt nothing. He fumbled with the bindings and knew it was hopeless.

He turned his back on the skis and the breaking ice and the distant storm and ran, ran until he could not remember a time when he had not fled over shifting ice, leaped over sudden black water, running toward a shore he no longer believed in, ice and distance and determination locked in mindless battle.

He ran without looking up from his outgoing trail, beating his nerveless hands against his shoulders, running until his beard was a thick white crust of exhaled breath, miles and hours of running until he could run no longer and his tears were ice on his cheeks.

And then he looked up and saw his cabin, warm brown against the blue-shadowed snow. He could run no more, but he did, across the bay, clawing up the ice foot, running toward the cabin as the white eternity dissolved around him.

Home and fire and life just ahead; just a few more steps and he was no longer running but leaning against the door, gasping and fumbling at the latch with rigid fingers until it swung inward, spilling him into the cabin. He had been away more than twelve hours, and the cabin was no warmer than the fjord ice. He must start the fire, start it in spite of hands that could not hold onto skis, much less matches.

He kicked the stove doors open and reached for the small box of matches on the shelf. Before he realized that he had touched it, the box flew off the shelf onto the floor. He heard the dry rattle of matches inside the box, and in his mind he saw them, buff wooden sticks and bulging red tips pregnant with fire.

He must have them.

He knelt in front of the stove and reached carefully for

Ice foot

the elusive box. Using one hand as a weight to hold the box in place, he tapped at the end with unfeeling fingers until the box flew open and matches fanned out across the floor.

But when he tried to pick up a match, his fingers were as useless as claws.

With an inarticulate cry of frustration, he beat his useless hands on his knees again and again and again. And felt nothing.

He went back to work on the matches. In time he discovered that he could pick up a match if he pushed the outer edges of his palms together like a clumsy vise. He carefully lifted the matchbox between his palms and wedged it between his knees. He squeezed down over the nearest match, worked the red head down, and swept it across the striking surface of the box. The match broke.

Slowly, patiently, he found and held another match, scraped it across carefully, saw it slip out from his palms. The third match dropped to the floor, and the fourth and the fifth. Each time he neither hesitated nor gave way to the feeling of futility that was as lethal as the cold. Finally a match flared to life.

With agonizing care he guided the tiny flame into the stove. The match landed in fine kindling, a tiny point of light in the dark stove. He held his breath for fear that the least draft would snuff out the vulnerable flame. A thin piece of kindling darkened, charred, then grew tiny points of blue flame. The pale tongues of light wavered, spread, burned red and orange and then gloriously gold.

The flames leaped incandescent.

Warmth spread across his face like a rising sun. He stayed motionless, kneeling in front of the stove, his eyes reflecting the miracle of fire.

He watched the flames for long moments, then rose and paced the cabin, arms flailing, trying to force blood into white fingers. When the room warmed enough, he struggled out of his wet clothes and rubbed himself as dry as his unfeeling fingers would allow. He pulled on warm clothes and resumed walking, beating his hands against his body every second step. He tried not to think about what would happen if his fingers were frozen beyond healing, the insidious gangrene that would spread and spread and be stopped only by self-amputation. Whatever the future brought, he knew he was supremely lucky to be alive.

Once he felt a faint tingling sensation, as though a feather had brushed over the back of his fingers. With growing hope he strode around the room, swinging his arms to force blood into his fingers, hands thumping against his shoulders.

With infinite slowness the tingling spread, became a subtle pulse of warmth. Gradually a feeling of heat crept across fingers that throbbed and throbbed and finally burst into pain. He stopped and held his hands in front of him, half expecting to see his fingers curling and charring from invisible flames.

But his fingers were like the land outside, cold and white, shadowed with blue.

He clamped his teeth and walked and beat his burning hands against his body until pain became a white blaze of agony. He kept walking, arms swinging ceaselessly, sweat gathering on his drawn face. When he could no longer endure it, he screamed and wept and cursed, his voice hoarse in the empty cabin. And he walked, swinging hands against shoulders, taking what comfort he could from the knowledge that the twisting agony meant his fingers still lived.

After four hours, agony became mere pain, and he was able to sleep. While he slept, thick blisters formed underneath his fingers, stretching from callused palms to fingertips. When he awoke, his fingers were almost immobile. He watched the blisters for long days, clumsy days when he could barely feed himself or the dogs.

In the evening of the seventh day, he sat in the light flooding through the window and pressed a sharp knife tip against a bulging blister. Clear serum oozed down the worn blade. He lifted the thick pad of white skin and saw a pink glow of healthy flesh. Carefully, patiently, he broke each blister. When all the fluid had drained away, he flexed his fingers experimentally. They were stiff, sensitive to the point of pain—and whole.

With an unconscious sigh, he picked up the knife and began paring away dead skin. As he worked, each finger emerged with a bright stripe of new flesh.

With a last hard pull, Ivar settled the bear hide over the sawhorse he had set up just outside of Main Cabin. He leaned over and moved his knife across the skin, scraping away bits of blubber. For three weeks he had roamed the fjord, looking for polar bears on the thinning ice, his fingers throbbing with cold. The weeks had been swift and beautiful and empty of white bear—until last night, when his huskies had burst into savage snarls beneath the midnight sun. Another bear that had been determined to eat huskies had now become a heavy white pelt underneath his flashing knife.

After awhile he stopped, flexed his fingers and looked toward the little bay just beyond the cabin. The ice was white and gray and sagging beneath the weight of a thousand hours of sunlight. Shallow pools and brine slicks glimmered through the crumbling cover of snow. Further out, near the center of the fjord, a ribbon of open water shone blue-black between wide white borders of ice.

Scattered along the shore and across the flatlands and high up on mountainsides, the first birds huddled in the snow, waiting for the melt, crying their impatience to the warm wind. They would not have to wait much longer. A new cycle was

Glaucous gulls waiting for the melt

gathering beneath ice and snow, drawing energy from the south wind and the high yellow sun.

He bent over the skin again, hearing the end of spring in the water dripping from cabin eaves. As he worked, the sounds of water faded beneath distant, twisting groans, birth pains of Fox River. He put aside his knife and listened as the river tested the strength of its winter womb. The sounds were urgent, stronger than yesterday, far stronger than the day before. He pulled on his mittens and began running toward the river.

The groans merged into long shrieks, then silence, then high screams as ice split away from rocky banks. By the time he reached the top of a slope overlooking the river, the first long cracks had radiated through the snow-covered ice.

He watched as snow pockets slumped inwards, vanished into sudden holes where water flowed unseen. The river rested, and the ice was silent for a long time. Then there were low moans, subtle shudders along the hidden river and finally a wild cannonade of shearing ice. With a prolonged, thunderous roar, Fox River ran down to the frozen sea.

As the echoes died, he watched blocks of ice ride on the back of the blue-green river, down and away, flowing over the shelf of Bear Bay in a pale turquoise fan. Soon the bay, too, would break up. The fan would spread and widen with each tide, sweeping ice before it, opening leads and channels until waves once again surged the length of the fjord, and a ship would come, riding the backs of swells from the distant sea. He would look up and see the ship, far off on the slate-blue water, waiting for him amid glacier calves floating low and cold and translucent.

Ivar watched, and knew his year-long day had ended.

Acknowledgment

Through all my years in Svalbard, from 1967 to 1973, I kept my diary up to date with a day-to-day description of happenings and discovery. I recorded in motion pictures and stills my way of living in the islands' unique natural conditions. The millions of birds in the sky. The polar bear, the fox and the reindeer on the frozen tundra. The seal, the fish and the crustaceans in the sea. All of them living in a perfect balance, preying and depending on each other for survival.

It was this gigantic theater, where I sat in the front row and saw, heard and felt the rules of nature, that made me stay year after year until I found my own part in the play.

As the pile of diary notes grew, a wish to pass my experiences to other people grew up along with it.

In the summer of 1973, everything was changed. Through the last two years, tourism, mining and the search for oil on the islands made headlines in the papers. Development came too fast, and the Norwegian government rushed into protection of wildlife and of certain areas, including Hornsund.

I left the islands, my cabins and all I had built up through years of hard work. Even if I did not understand the policy in excluding one man from his area, when oil companies and other groups kept their rights almost unlimited wherever they had staked their claims. The fast-growing developments certainly called for protection, but I did my share by moving out with mixed feelings. I could get along with the Arctic environment, but not with the growing bureaucracy.

Back in Oslo, Norway, my movie *One Year in the Arctic* was shown on Norwegian television, which brought me to

London. There I met Eve Arnold and Stephany Bennett, who became important links in the chain that brought me to *The Year-Long Day*.

In California, my good friend Guy Greengard gave me help and encouragement every time I paced his guest-room floor in search of English words that would explain what I wanted to say in my native tongue.

Through the demolishing mist that had slowly built up in my mind, after six months of struggle with a second language, came Ann and Evan Maxwell. Loaded with new spirit.

Immediate contact between us, their love and understanding for nature as big as mine, a growing friendship that kept us together when things got rough through hundreds of hours of conversation and work—all these resulted in *The Year-Long Day*.

Thank you, Ann. . . . Thank you, Evan. . . . What started as my life is our book now. You wrote it with me; I lived it once more with you. Thank you, everyone involved.

O. Ivar Ruud